DISCARDED

The Dynamics of Electrical Energy Supply and Demand

R. K. Pachauri

The Praeger Special Studies program—utilizing the most modern and efficient book production techniques and a selective worldwide distribution network—makes available to the academic, government, and business communities significant, timely research in U.S. and international economic, social, and political development.

The Dynamics of Electrical Energy Supply and Demand

An Economic Analysis

Praeger Publishers   New York   Washington   London

Library of Congress Cataloging in Publication Data

Pachauri, R K
   The dynamics of electrical energy supply and demand.

   (Praeger special studies in U.S. economic, social, and political issues)

   1. Electric utilities--United States. 2. Economic forecasting--United States.   I. Title.
HD9685.U5P27   338.4'7'36320973   75-19806
ISBN 0-275-01530-0

PRAEGER PUBLISHERS
111 Fourth Avenue, New York, N.Y. 10003, U.S.A.

Published in the United States of America in 1975
by Praeger Publishers, Inc.

All rights reserved

© 1975 by Praeger Publishers, Inc.

Printed in the United States of America

To my parents

Dr. and Mrs. A. R. Pachauri

FOREWORD
Edward W. Erickson

A large measure of the responsibility for what has come to be called the "energy crisis" must be assigned to United States regulatory and policy failures. This is true, for example, with regard to the events which led to the explosion of world oil prices, the onerousness of gasoline lines, and the shortages of natural gas. It is particularly true for the utilities sector.

Not only is the utilities sector subject to regulatory failures in other energy sectors which then translate into higher fuel prices, but the utilities sector is also subject to a form of direct regulation which is peculiar to it. This regulation, and the regulatory lag which is endemic to it, have complicated the problems faced by the utilities sector. In fairness to the regulatory authorities, however, they are often not personally responsible for the sense of crisis which has afflicted electric utility rate proceedings. State regulatory agencies often operate with creaky regulatory machinery, inadequate staffs, and in a gale force storm of impinging and conflicting claims and counterclaims. In addition, the utility sector itself must bear some of the responsibility for the current state of affairs.

In utility rate proceedings, "regulatory lag" is now universally used as a pejorative word by utility company witnesses. "Regulatory lag," in this context, refers to several things. First, cases piled up as utilities petitioned for rate relief. Companies which, for the last quarter of a century, might have filed a rate case once every five or ten years were now petitioning for rate relief on a back-to-back basis. As soon as one case was decided, another was filed. Moreover, the cases were controversial. Rates were going up—and going up more for some than for others. Not only were more utilities seeking rate relief more often, but the number of intervenors in each case also increased. The inevitable result of all this was that the average elapsed time between when a case was filed and when it was decided stretched out. This is one aspect of regulatory lag.

Another aspect of regulatory lag which has perplexed utility management and nearly everyone else concerned with utility regulation is inflation. Utility rates are set on the basis of analysis of data from a "test period." This test period is often a historical, though recent, period of time which ended just prior to the beginning of the rate case. During an inflationary era, these past costs based upon a historical test period are an imperfect guide to what costs now are. The problem is, however, that historical costs have an actual—though often not undisputed—basis in fact which is denied to unaudited present costs or projected future costs.

If the revenue requirements necessary to generate the allowed rate of return are based upon a past period's operating costs, then in a situation where inflationary pressure is forcing operating costs up across the board, the allowed rate of return will never be attained. If inflation continues or accelerates, the comparison between future and past costs worsens and actual rates of return fall even further short of the allowed rate of return. Inflation is one contributing component to earnings attrition and the effects of inflation are another aspect of regulatory lag.

Earnings attrition is not a function of inflation alone. In recent years, utilities have had increasing difficulty in earning their allowed rate of return. Moreover, the shortfall between the allowed and the actual rate of return has tended to increase as time elapses after a rate case. In addition to inflation, another major contributing factor to earnings attrition is the economic law of demand. It is not news that in the last few years electric utility rates have risen dramatically. The principle of the economic law of demand is that, other things equal, the higher the price of any commodity, the less is demanded.

The law of demand and higher prices contribute to earnings attrition in the following way. If a utility is expected to sell X gigawatt hours of electricity and if its rates are set so that the earnings from the sale of those X gigawatt hours will yield it the allowed rate of return, then if the utility sells only .9X gigawatt hours, its earnings will be insufficient to yield it the allowed rate of return. If the price of electricity is rising rapidly and substantially, the economic law of demand operates to turn expected sales of X gigawatt hours into .9X. Even if anticipated inflationary effects upon costs were perfectly adjusted for, demand changes due to higher prices would contribute to earnings attrition unless the price responsiveness of demand is carefully taken into account.

An indication of the effect of higher prices upon electricity consumption can be had from examining the following table. The comparisons of particular interest are those which deal with the reductions in the rate of growth of demand between 1972-73 and 1973-74. Higher prices are not the only factors at work in these demand growth rate changes. The effects of the weather, the recession and public-spirited, voluntary, non-price induced conservation are also contained in these numbers. But the numbers in the table below are illustrative of the potential demand swings—in part price induced—which must be taken into account by utility companies, utility commissioners and their staffs, and others in planning for the electric generation and consumption sector of the United States energy economy.

Load growth in the Southeast fell from a rate of growth of +10.0 percent for 1972-73 to -0.5 percent for 1973-74. Peak demand growth slowed markedly. For the 1972-73 interval, six of the twelve months showed double-digit growth factors. For the 1973-74 interval, only one month showed a double-digit peak demand growth factor—and that month was lower than five of the months for the 1972-73 interval. Moreover, three of the months in the 1973-74 interval actually had negative peak demand growth.

In this regard, the peak demand growth for August declined from +10.4 percent to +2.3 percent from 1972-73 to 1973-74. In addition, load growth actually turned around for the December-February period. For these three months, the sum of the three month-by-month load growth figures for the 1972-73 period was +32.1 percent. The corresponding figure for 1973-74 was -10.1 percent. January alone had a swing of 24.7 percentage points—from +18.0 percent to -6.7 percent. These peak demand and load growth numbers suggest substantial price sensitivity for electricity demand.

The indication of substantial price sensitivity is confirmed by looking at the comparisons across regions. In general, the peak demand and load growth were reduced most in those regions which had the largest price increases for electricity. Conversely, reductions in the growth of peak demand and total load were least in those areas in which prices increased least. This again suggests substantial price sensitivity. Such demand response in conjunction with regulatory lag can have a marked effect upon earnings attrition.

It must be noted that regulatory lag was not always a pejorative word from the standpoint of utility company officials and witnesses. In fact, the phrase was seldom heard to pass their lips. But regulatory lag has always been at work.

The total profits of a utility are a function of its rate base and its actual rate of return. If fuel prices are stable and a firm can add to its rate base a new generating plant that has higher operating efficiencies than the older (historical test period) equipment upon which the revenue requirements for its allowed rate of return were based, then it can increase its total profit. It has an incentive to grow. The longer the period between rate cases, the greater the possibility to take advantage of such a situation.

Rate structures were designed to foster growth. A good deal of attention has recently been focused upon declining block rate structures, but the crucial aspect of the induced growth component in electric utility rate structure designs has been cross-subsidization among customer classes which have either more or less price responsive demands. If judicious balancing of gains and losses in growth potential could be made to result in a net gain of a percentage

MAJOR SYSTEMS REGIONAL LOAD DATA
1973 versus 1972 (12 Months) and
1974 versus 1973 (12 Months)

SOUTHEAST REGION—III

	Energy for Load Gigawatt Hours			Peak Demand Megawatts		
	1972 (12 months)	1973 (12 months)	Percent Change	1972 (12 months)	1973 (12 months)	Percent Change
January	28,082.7	33,143.8	+18.0	53,545.2	60,689.0	+13.3
February	27,530.2	30,065.2	+9.2	53,713.1	60,387.1	+12.4
March	26,917.7	29,288.6	+8.8	48,510.6	53,191.9	+9.7
April	23,453.1	27,963.0	+9.9	48,484.0	52,910.5	+9.1
May	26,543.8	29,470.3	+11.0	48,688.0	55,478.0	+13.9
June	28,959.1	33,267.7	+14.9	56,107.8	63,190.8	+12.6
July	32,056.9	35,843.7	+11.8	62,175.6	66,738.2	+7.3
August	33,637.5	36,243.6	+7.7	61,221.8	67,559.4	+10.4
September	30,554.4	33,554.5	+9.8	59,699.0	65,598.0	+9.9
October	28,354.2	31,968.6	+12.7	53,234.9	61,043.0	+14.7
November	29,234.9	29,790.1	+1.9	54,710.4	56,176.9	+2.7
December	30,713.8	32,206.7	+4.9	57,924.2	62,356.4	+7.7
Total U.S.	348,038.3	382,805.8	+10.0			

	1973 (12 months)	1974 (12 months)	Percent Change	1973 (12 months)	1974 (12 months)	Percent Change
January	33,143.8	30,936.6	-6.7	60,689.0	56,919.5	-6.2
February	30,065.2	29,407.7	-2.2	60,387.1	62,572.2	+3.6
March	29,288.6	29,939.4	+2.2	53,191.9	57,113.7	+7.4
April	27,963.0	28,740.2	+2.8	52,910.5	55,425.7	+4.8
May	29,470.2	31,451.0	+6.7	55,478.0	61,646.8	+11.1
June	33,267.7	32,429.2	-2.5	63,190.8	65,786.2	+4.1
July	35,843.7	36,328.3	+1.4	66,738.2	68,478.0	+2.6
August	36,243.6	36,701.5	+1.3	67,559.4	69,118.0	+2.3
September	33,554.5	32,853.2	-2.1	65,598.0	66,186.0	+0.9
October	31,968.6	30,545.3	-4.5	61,043.0	57,122.0	-6.4
November	29,790.1	29,755.5	-0.1	56,176.9	56,952.0	+1.4
December	32,206.7	31,815.0	-1.2	62,356.4	61,226.0	-1.8
Total U.S.	382,805.2	380,902.9	-0.5			

Source: <u>FPC News</u>, Vol. 8, No. 13 (week ended March 28, 1975), p. 36.

point or so in the overall system growth rate, then the inexorable effect of compound interest would be a powerful tool for managements with time horizons which are measured in decades.* In this situation, regulatory lag was a term reserved for academic economists.

If and as inflation slows, fuel costs stabilize (and automatic fuel cost adjustment clauses are incorporated into rate designs), the recession ends, and consumers adjust to new and higher electricity prices, there may be some tendency for a reemergence of complacency and neglect for rate structure issues. Such complacency and neglect would not be benign. It is unlikely that we will ever be able to muddle through in the future in the same ways as we did in the past.

This is why the following book is an important contribution to the literature. It is the beginning of a series of efforts which must be carried on within and without electric utility company staffs. These efforts must focus upon the systematic interrelationships among all the short-run and long-run components of the demand for electricity. This focus must include all customer classes and total load and peak demands. The time is at hand when utility managements, regulators, and energy planners must understand the characteristics of electricity demand as well as the utility companies now understand the cost basis for their sophisticated load dispatch decisions. Such knowledge is a prerequisite both for future rational policy making and for working ourselves out of the consequences of past policy failures.

---

*There is an unfortunate general tendency for uncritical observers to ascribe the motivating factor for growth to the operation of the free enterprise system. The TVA, public universities, the U.S.S.R. and the federal bureaucracy are black swans in counterpoint to this naivete. To be sure, the brief sketch here of one of the facilitating mechanisms for growth focuses upon the operation of the private profit motive. But the broader questions are those of the rate and composition of <u>worthwhile</u> growth and the force and direction of the private sector within a mixed economy.

PREFACE

The author's interest in the electric power industry was first aroused when studying the economic considerations involved in changing from diesel and steam to electric traction on a railroad system. Subsequently, the author researched the area more deeply in 1971-72 while developing a dynamic simulation model for forecasting electrical energy demand. This model, dealing with a small region in western North Carolina, was developed to fulfill the thesis requirements for a master of science degree at the North Carolina State University, Raleigh. A larger model using regression techniques for estimation and synthesized with systems dynamics simulation methodology was later built as part of the author's dissertation research for a doctorate in the fields of economics and industrial engineering. This model was applicable to the entire region served by Carolina Power and Light Company, and although some policy functions with feedback effects were built into it, its primary purpose was to forecast the time path of demand for the region.

With a model as limited in purpose as this, it was somewhat uncomfortable to accept the boundaries drawn around it. A deeper study into the economics of the electric utility industry showed clearly that a study of demand alone could not be carried out faithfully without relating it to the supply of electrical energy, and the other way around. In the summer of 1974 an effort was made, therefore, to construct a fuller and completely revised model covering both supply and demand and using the earlier work done for the doctoral study, as well as a great deal of new material collected from various sources.

In an endeavor of this type it is difficult to name all those to whom the author is indebted. First and foremost, sincere thanks and immense appreciation are due to the co-chairman and members of the author's doctoral committee—Professors R. W. Llewellyn, B. M. Olsen, L. A. Ihnen, and R. H. Bernhard. Without their understanding, help, and encouragement this study would not have been possible. A special expression of gratitude is reserved for Professor E. W. Erickson, who gave his valuable time in guiding and offering very useful advice on the work being done, at every stage of the project. Any flaws and shortcomings, however, are the sole responsibility of the author.

The author also benefited from valuable discussions with officials of Carolina Power and Light Company. In particular, Archie Futrell, Dr. Ben McConnell, and Mrs. June Jones were very helpful in furthering the author's interests. Officials of the North Carolina Utilities Commission at Raleigh are also due a large measure of sincere thanks for making available a fund of data related to the Carolina Power and Light system. In particular, the author wishes to express his deep gratitude to Bill Irish for his help and initiative in providing such data.

Messrs. Cone-Heiden were very kind in permitting duplication of some of the diagrams in their book <u>Power Generation Alternatives</u> for use in these pages. Mrs. Linda Collins is deserving of the author's deep gratitude and genuine admiration for typing the manuscript in record time, in addition to carrying on her normal duties.

Last, but not least, the author would like to express his "unbiased" appreciation to his wife, Saroj, and daughters, Rashmi, Shona, and Moneesha, who displayed perfect understanding and tact toward a disagreeable stranger who suddenly appeared in the home during the writing of this book.

CONTENTS

	Page
FOREWORD, Edward W. Erickson	vii
PREFACE	xiii
LIST OF TABLES	xviii
LIST OF FIGURES	xx
INTRODUCTION	xxii

Part I: THE DEMAND FOR ELECTRICAL ENERGY

INTRODUCTION TO PART I	3
Note	5

Chapter

1	SURVEY OF EXISTING STUDIES AND MODELS	6
	Notes	21
2	DEVELOPMENT OF A SUITABLE FORECASTING METHODOLOGY	23
	The Systems Dynamics Concept	23
	Model Specification	27
	Residential Sector	27
	Industrial Sector	33
	Commercial Sector	35
	Statistical Methods	36
	Description of the Dynamic Simulation Model	49
	Domestic Sector	51
	Industrial Sector	54
	Commercial Sector	56
	Notes	58

Chapter	Page

3 SIMULATION RESULTS — 59

    Forecast up to 1990 — 59
    Sensitivity Analysis — 67

Part II: THE SUPPLY OF ELECTRICAL ENERGY

INTRODUCTION TO PART II — 81

    Note — 83

4 POWER GENERATION ALTERNATIVES — 84

    Hydroelectric Generation — 84
    Conventional Steam-Powered Generation — 87
    Internal Combustion Turbine Generation — 92
    Nuclear Power Generation — 92
    Notes — 97

5 THE ECONOMICS OF ELECTRICITY SUPPLY — 98

    A Theoretical Framework — 99
    Hydroelectric Generation — 101
    Conventional Steam-Electric Generation — 103
    Gas Turbine Generation — 107
    Nuclear Generation — 110
    An Illustrative Example in Capacity Planning — 113
    The Economic Benefits of Coordination — 121
    Transmission and Distribution Costs — 125
    Notes — 126

6 ELECTRIC UTILITY FINANCE — 128

    Notes — 134

Part III: POLICY ALTERNATIVES FOR THE FUTURE

INTRODUCTION TO PART III — 137

Chapter		Page
7	INTERACTIONS BETWEEN SUPPLY AND DEMAND	138
	Note	147
8	THE RESTRUCTURING OF ELECTRIC RATES	148
	Note	157
9	THE CASE FOR GOVERNMENT ASSISTANCE	158
	Notes	162
10	THE OUTLOOK FOR THE UNITED STATES	163
	Notes	171
ABOUT THE AUTHOR		173

LIST OF TABLES

Table		Page
2.1	Estimation of Customers in High Consumption Group	38
2.2	Estimation of Customers in Medium Consumption Group	39
2.3	Estimation of Birth Rate	42
2.4	Estimation of Migration	43
2.5	Estimation of Business Subgroup Customers	46
2.6	Estimation of School Subgroup Customers	46
2.7	Estimation of Church Subgroup Customers	47
2.8	Estimation of Housing Subgroup Customers	47
2.9	Estimation of Construction Subgroup Customers	48
II.1	Percentage Breakdown of Costs of Electricity Supplied in the United States	81
II.2	Construction Expenditures—Investor-Owned Electric Utilities Excluding Alaska and Hawaii	82
4.1	Average Number of Neutrons Emitted per Neutron Absorbed by the Fuel	95
5.1	Capital Cost of Typical Conventional Hydroelectric Projects	102
5.2	Conventional Steam-Electric Plant Data for Selected Years from 1938-72	103
5.3	Investments in Conventional Steam-Powered Generation in the United States	105
5.4	Percentages of Different Fossil Fuels Used in Steam-Powered Generation in the United States	108

Table		Page
5.5	Cost of Fossil-Fuels Burned for Steam-Powered Generation in the United States	108
5.6	Annual Generating Costs for Conventional Steam-Powered Plants in the United States	109
5.7	New Capacity Additions Announced in the United States for 300 Megawatts and Above	110
5.8	Estimates of Exploitable Resources of Uranium	112
5.9	Kilowatt Capacity Required for Meeting Future Demand	115
6.1	Capitalization Ratios Expressed as Percentages—All U.S. Investor-Owned Electric Utilities	130
6.2	Weighted Average of Earnings—Moody's 24 Utility Common Stocks	130
6.3	Average Yields on Moody's A and Baa Rated Bonds	134
7.1	Data on Future Capacity Addition Plan for the Carolina Power and Light System	140
7.2	Interaction Between Demand, Investment Planning, and Financial Status	142
7.3	Effect of Varying Electricity Prices on Future Financial Operations of the Utility	145
8.1	Effect of Seasonal Pricing	152
8.2	Effects of Changes in Rate Structure Applicable to the Residential Sector	156
8.3	Effect of Revised Rates on Kilowatt Hour per Customer in the Residential Sector	156

LIST OF FIGURES

Figure		Page
1.1	Price-Quantity Relationship with Elastic Demand for Electricity	7
1.2	Price-Quantity Relationship with Inelastic Demand for Electricity	8
2.1	Structure of Lagged Effects of Prices and Incomes	30
2.2	Flow Chart for One Rate Group in the Residential Sector	52
2.3	Flow Chart for One Industry Group in the Industrial Sector	55
2.4	Flow Chart for the Commercial Sector	57
3.1	Effect of Varying Regional Growth with Low Income per Capita	68
3.2	Effect of Varying Regional Growth with Low Electricity Prices on Total Migration	68
3.3	Effect of Varying Regional Growth with Low Electricity Prices on Total Population	69
3.4	Effect of Varying Regional Growth with Low Electricity Prices on Total Demand in Residential Sector	69
3.5	Effect of Varying Regional Growth with Low Electricity Prices on Total Demand in Commercial Sector	70
3.6	Effect of Varying Regional Growth with High Electricity Prices on Total Demand in Residential Sector	70
3.7	Effect of Varying Regional Growth with High Electricity Prices on Total Demand in Commercial Sector	71

Figure		Page
3.8	Effect of Varying National Growth on U.S. per Capita Income	72
3.9	Effect of Varying National Growth on Regional Migration	73
3.10	Effect of Varying National Growth on Regional Population	73
3.11	Effect of Varying National Growth on Total Demand in Residential Sector	74
3.12	Effect of Varying National Growth on Total Demand in Commercial Sector	74
3.13	Effect of Varying Prices on Total Demand in Residential Sector	75
3.14	Effect of Varying Prices on Total Demand in Commercial Sector	76
3.15	Effect of Varying Prices on Total Demand in Industrial Sector	76
4.1	Distribution of Storage Capacity Between Different Plants in Series	86
4.2	Load-Sharing Between Plants on the Same River	86
4.3	Coal-Fired Plant Mass Balance	89
4.4	Oil-Fired Plant Mass Balance	90
4.5	Gas-Fired Plant Mass Balance	91
4.6	Single-Cycle Reactor System	93
4.7	Schematic Flow Diagram of High-Temperature Gas-Cooled Reactor Plant	96
5.1	Relationship Between Plant Costs and Unit Sizes	105

INTRODUCTION

    This book attempts to develop an interdisciplinary approach in the study of the electric power industry in the United States of America. The main emphasis in this endeavor has been placed on studying and explaining the dynamic behavior of the market for electrical energy. The subject matter presented in the ensuing pages takes a long term view of the electric utility industry, even though the current debate between government and industry seems to be centering on what policies to adopt to solve the short run problems of the industry. What is written hopefully will be of more than topical interest, since what started some years ago as an energy crisis has come to stay mainly as an electrical energy crisis.

    A large amount of research has been done and learned publications have been produced in this vital area, but the large bulk of work has not exposed some of the dynamic influences at play in the system. This has been so mainly because most research on the economics of the electric power business has attempted to deal with aggregation, covering, in most cases, the United States as a whole. This naturally has been accomplished at the cost of sacrificing some measure of detail that is possible when only the operations of a single utility are being modeled. The structure of the electric utility industry in the United States is characterized by a great degree of industrial uniformity. Since the commercial supply of electric power in this country is regulated by designated public agencies, there are certain constraints that typify the behavior of a utility as a part of a distinct entity.

    This study of the dynamics of electrical supply and demand is based on a detailed model of the region served by Carolina Power and Light Company, extending over parts of North and South Carolina. The choice of this particular utility's area of operation was not based on mere convenience and accessibility to information but on the outstanding record that has been achieved by Carolina Power and Light among all the utilities of the nation. In the January 1, 1974 issue of <u>Forbes</u>[1] magazine, Carolina Power and Light was listed as being the fastest growing electric utility in the country. In 1973, it was also given the distinction of being the most outstanding utility in the United States by <u>Electric Light and Power</u> magazine. The management of this utility is held in high esteem in industry circles and its senior executives have been involved actively in evolution of national power policies through participation in various committees and professional bodies.

It was felt that by tracing through the dynamic effects of market phenomena on an individual utility's operations it may be possible to gain insight into the time-varying behavior of the industry much in the same way as the study of microeconomic principles is essential in understanding aggregate macroeconomic activity. In fact, the approach used is much stronger than is indicated by this analogy, since the region used as the basic model is a much larger share of the total than would be the model of a single firm in the economic activity of the nation. In expanding the implications from this region-specific study to embrace the total electrical energy sector of the United States, the author believed that there would only be differences in degree between the conclusions derived for the Carolina region and those that perhaps could be obtained specifically for other regions in the country.

The demand and supply relationships in the electric power business are undergoing an important test during present times. This country and much of the industrialized world have seen a prolonged period of steadily extending trends and patterns in electrical energy consumption that accompanied steady trends in economic growth, population, and prices of electricity and its substitutes. Electric utilities throughout the nation enjoyed a fairly long spell of financially sound operations that were brought about by significant reductions in costs of power generation through technological innovations and substantial economies of scale. The entire industry in this period became attuned to an operating environment in which sudden changes in market conditions were conspicuously absent. The philosophy and practice of management that developed in this period was directed only toward dealing with problems of growth imposed on their systems. This has changed, but much to the misfortune of the industry the transformation has not been easy or smooth.

The current spate of problems facing the suppliers of electric power in this country, contrary to popular belief, did not originate with the tremendous spurt in oil prices brought about in the wake of the 1973 Arab-Israeli war. These problems had come to stay and merely were accentuated by the oil price developments of the next two years. As early as 1970, the National Power Survey had pointed toward a possible reduction in demand in the future as a result of higher electricity prices. In that year itself a change in electricity prices became evident. There was also an increase in commitments for capital expenditures, partly as a result of increases in construction costs of conventional steam plants, but the main financial impact that was felt was due to larger outlays in nuclear generating potential. According to the Edison Electric Institute's Statistical Year Book for 1973,[2] total construction expenditures made by investor-owned electric utilities in 1973 were $14.9 billion, compared with $10.145 billion in 1970 and $6.12 billion in 1967. This indicates that within a period of six years construction expenditures had more than doubled.

In an industry not subjected to frequent and radical changes in demand patterns, the presence of long lags in policy making and readjustment of expansion plans is not unexpected. Besides, the very nature and timing of investments required for electric power generation makes this a feature that cannot and must not react to sudden changes in behavior of the market. An evaluation of long run trends is essential before any changes in investment plans can be made. To that extent one could even contend that the abnormal increase in oil prices thrust on the world by the Organization of Petroleum Exporting Companies (OPEC) in the long run would prove beneficial to the industry by drawing attention to the need for constant evaluation criteria in investment planning. There is little reason to believe that in the absence of a severe crisis similar to today's, government and utility managements would have made serious efforts to reorient policies and plans for the future.

Although positive changes, such as price, have worked to the detriment of the electric power business, the cessation of other changes experienced in the past also has acted adversely on the industry. An example of this can be seen from the fact that technological changes in power generation, which accounted for lower generating costs in the 1950s, had leveled off by the middle of the 1960s. Despite increasing prices of fuels from 1940 to 1970, the cost of fuel per kilowatt hour (KwH) remained remarkably stable, amounting to a reduction in real terms. This was brought about by changes in plant design and economies of scale. Fuel prices from 1940 to 1970 had increased by a total of 120 percent. In the same period the cost of fuel per KwH increased by only 50 percent and in 1965 was actually at almost the same level as in 1940. This was a direct result of improvements in the average heat rate. Whereas in 1951 the heat rate for the electric utility industry was at an average of 13,641 British thermal units (Btu) per kilowatt hour, it dropped to 10,552 in 1961 and to 10,536 in 1971. This indicates that fuel efficiency reached a plateau during the 1960s; subsequent improvements, too, in this aspect of power generation have been of a minor nature.

The institutional framework modeled in this study is that of investor-owned electric utilities in the United States. There are two basic justifications for this approach. First, the investor-owned electric utilities in the United States supply an overwhelming share of electrical energy used in the nation. In 1973 this sector of the industry generated almost 75 percent of the total energy supplied in the United States. Also, the investor-owned utilities in the nation controlled approximately 79 percent of the total generating capacity in 1973. A number of projections made for the future show that this share is likely to increase in the 1980s and 1990s. There is justification, therefore, for studying the behavior of this sector of our economy in detail. The second justification stems from the fact that the problems being faced in this sector cross institutional boundaries. The dynamic behavior exhibited by the market for electric power in the United States is common to different units within the industry, any differences observed being only a matter of degree. Public-owned power suppliers have been experiencing the same problems and have been subjected to the same forces that have been at work on the private sector of the industry. The choice of a particular region served by an investor-owned electric utility in our model, it is believed for these reasons, would be largely representative of the entire industry as a whole.

The subject matter in this book has been organized into three parts. Part I deals with the demand for electrical energy and occupies the largest number of pages. This was found necessary because subsequent investigation into the supply side of the industry takes off necessarily from the demand for electricity. The development of a suitable model for demand is essential to a study of the dynamics of any industry, and hence the author carefully carried out a detailed survey of literature in the field before describing his own model for electrical energy demand. In developing the discussion of this model, the author has taken a step-by-step approach in first establishing the methodology used, then explaining the economic basis used in the specification of the model, and finally explaining the estimation of relationships used in the model. The use of the model in simulating the period up to 1990 and arriving at forecasts of the dynamic time path of demand has been described by explaining some of the features of the systems dynamics computer program used.

Part II provides a broad overview of the technical choices available in power generation and follows this up with some of the economic features associated with each alternative. The model developed in Part I is then modified to yield some outputs that are used to discuss an appropriate methodology for making choices between different alternative combinations of generating plant. A brief note is provided on the nature of transmission and distribution costs associated with the supply of electric power, but the treatment centers mainly on choices in generation only. Part II concludes with a discussion of electric utility finances and the financial crisis facing the entire electric utility industry today.

Part III of this book deals with and tests various policy options available for stabilizing the industry and for ensuring a nationwide supply of electric power at prices that would not increase rapidly enough to cause serious dislocations to the economy and its constituent parts. For this purpose, the dynamic model used earlier was extended considerably further to include financial variables for the utility and to permit an explicit treatment of rate structures and pricing policies.

Implications derived from a series of simulation runs carried out with the extended model were then used to discuss policy options that should be considered at the national level. The final chapter discusses in summary form the state of the electrical energy sector in the United States and some comments are offered on what, according to the author, is an overview of future developments, based on the study carried out by him and described in these pages.

NOTES

1. "Sixth Annual Report on American Industry," *Forbes* (January 1, 1974): 185.
2. Edison Electric Institute, *Statistical Year Book of the Electric Utility Industry for 1973* (New York: Edison Electric Institute, 1974).

PART

I

**THE DEMAND
FOR ELECTRICAL
ENERGY**

INTRODUCTION
TO PART I

In this part of the book we will investigate and analyze the determinants of demand for electrical energy and, further, develop a methodology for arriving at dynamic forecasts of demand. To a large degree the present crisis being faced by major electric utilities in the United States is a crisis in forecasting demand and in correctly identifying and assessing the effects thereon of various economic and demographic factors. Most utilities experienced a prolonged period of steady growth in demand since World War II and consequently determined that forecasting methods in the "naive" category served their needs remarkably well. In most cases utility forecasters have been merely extrapolating past trends to obtain fairly reliable forecasts. This approach worked well until recently, mainly because

(1) there were no major changes in trends exhibited by influencing factors during the 1960s (prices of fuel oil, coal, gas, and electricity, respectively, and income per capita maintained fairly steady trends during this period);

(2) power generation was largely dependent on the use of fossil fuels. Power plants employing these technologies had short gestation periods and reached full capacity generation in three to five years. Thus, errors in forecasting could be corrected by relatively quick installation and commissioning of additional capacity.

Significant changes did take place, however, with respect to both these features in the early 1970s. Trends in population growth, which were in the 1960s under the influence of the postwar "baby boom," changed quite suddenly. Trends in electricity prices started changing as early as 1970, but their increases truly were unprecedented in 1973 and 1974. The following figures up to 1973, extracted from the Statistical Year Book of the Edison Electric Institute,[1] illustrate this new trend of increasing real prices of electrical energy:

Year	Electricity Price Index	Consumer Price Index
1973	124.9	133.1
1972	118.9	125.3
1971	113.2	121.3
1970	106.2	116.3
1969	102.8	109.8
1968	100.9	104.2

Year	Electricity Price Index	Consumer Price Index
1967	100.0	100.0
1966	99.1	97.2
1965	99.1	94.5
1964	99.6	92.9

The development of nuclear technology now necessitates the evolution of suitable forecasting methodologies. Most electric utilities today find that from the decision to invest in a nuclear plant to the time it becomes fully operational, a period of 10 to 12 years elapses in meeting various institutional constraints and environmental studies and following construction schedules, which are often hampered by technical and financial problems. Some of these are discussed in a later part of this book. However, despite these problems and, increasingly, because of the expected ascent of other fuel prices, nuclear power generation today represents an outstanding economic choice for adoption on a large scale in this nation. As an essential input into long range decision making for investments in nuclear power, it is imperative that forecasting methodologies be suitable for long range demand predictions.

An equally important offshoot of this imperative lies in the fact that the determinants of demand are much too complex to remain unchanged over the range of such a long term forecast. Population, income, industrial growth, and commercial activities are nebulous factors that render any electricity demand forecast rather weak. The enlightened planner for an electric utility is concerned, therefore, not just with a single set of forecasts for the future, but prefers to use a range of outcomes associated with various trends that can be visualized in the movement of these factors. As such, forecasting methodology that could serve U.S. electric utilities most suitably must therefore be capable of

(1) providing reliable forecasts based on a reasonable set of assumptions related to major factors influencing demand for electrical energy, and

(2) illustrating clearly the behavior of the system that determines demand, particularly in response to changes in assumptions related to the values of the determining factors.

This second feature is most important in the context of the current electric utility crisis in the United States. Faced with a failure in forecasting, and constrained by a commitment of funds and resources for construction of nuclear plants, utilities can only solve their problems by a careful analysis of new long term policy options. This can only be done if an integrated dynamic model, embodying important intercomponent relationships and feedback effects in the system, is used to study the effects through time of a set of policy alternatives.

It is with this objective that the following chapters present the development of a dynamic model for demand for an individual utility. As mentioned earlier, the appropriate framework for studying the problem of electrical energy supply and demand is from the viewpoint of a typical utility. The future of electrical energy developments in this country is in the hands of utility executives. The government merely can be regarded as an exogenous force, which by its actions can at best influence the decisions of the utility policy makers; but under our current institutional arrangement, the utilities' actions can only be regulated and not dictated. The model developed in this part of the book is later used for studying the dynamic interactions between supply and demand and the testing of various policy alternatives, which must be evaluated under the crisis conditions prevailing today.

The demand model is developed and described in some detail, following a survey of work done in the field. This survey is provided to lay the groundwork for some of the microeconomic considerations involved in the specification of the dynamic model and to present to the interested reader a critique of existing models in the literature.

NOTE

1. Edison Electric Institute, <u>Statistical Year Book of the Electric Utility Industry for 1973</u> (New York: Edison Electric Institute, 1974),

CHAPTER 1

SURVEY OF EXISTING STUDIES AND MODELS

Before entering into a survey of literature in this field, it would be relevant to discuss some of the conceptual problems involved in estimating demand for electricity. These arise mainly because most utilities offer their customers electricity at declining block rates. Considering, for instance, an individual household, the supply curve facing it would be of the type shown as SS in Figure 1.1. D_0, D_1, and D_2 represent different positions of the household's demand curve. When a shift in this curve takes place from D_0 to D_1 and D_1 to D_2, on account of, say, an increase in income, then the increase in consumption will consist of two effects. The first would measure a shift in the demand curve itself increasing the quantity consumed from Q_0 to Q_1' at the original price. The second effect takes place because of a lower price now offered to the household as a result of increased consumption at Q_1'. This second effect results in a further increase in consumption from Q_1' to Q_1 and represents a movement along the demand curve from A to B. Similar effects are produced when the demand curve shifts from D_1 to D_2.

The phenomenon described above presents a serious problem in estimation, because in specifying a model for demand, in addition to including all the factors that cause a shift in the demand curve itself, it is essential to specify the supply function as well. In the absence of such a complete specification, the increase in quantity demanded from Q_1' to Q_1, as a result of the price drop from A to B, cannot be identified. In other words, the demand curve cannot be estimated correctly.

Until recently it was generally believed, particularly by the electric utilities themselves, that price had no significant effect on demand for electricity. Evidence of a negative relationship between

EXISTING STUDIES AND MODELS 7

FIGURE 1.1

Price-Quantity Relationship with Elastic Demand
for Electricity

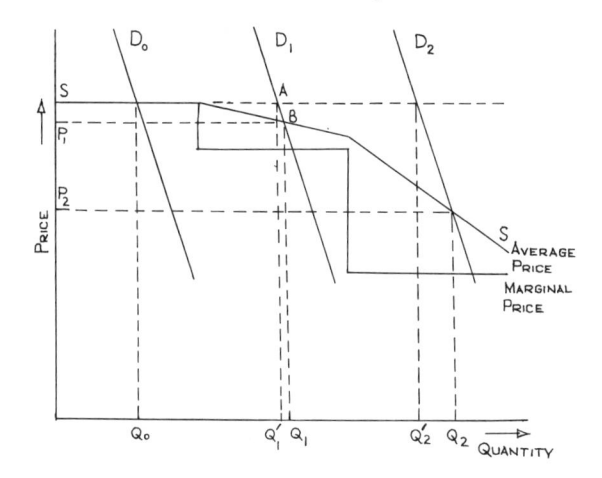

Source: Compiled by author.

price and quantity demanded was explained away as the effect of shifts in the demand curve on price due to a declining rate structure, rather than the effect of price on quantity demanded. This can be viewed in terms of a supply schedule similar to that in Figure 1.1. This schedule is shown in conjunction with a set of inelastic demand curves in Figure 1.2. Proponents of the inelastic demand view contend that even with inelastic demand curves, as shown in Figure 1.2, a negative price-quantity relationship is obtained because of the shape of the supply schedule. Some of the studies to be discussed below have shown this view to be untrue.

Another problem peculiar to electricity demand estimation arises once again out of the declining rate structure. In the economic world, given perfect market conditions, the quantity to be consumed is determined by comparing the marginal benefit from every additional unit consumed with its marginal price. However, as can be seen from Figures 1.1 and 1.2, there is a divergence between marginal and average prices of electricity and generally data on marginal prices are not available for estimation purposes. Thus most studies in this field necessarily have had to use average prices instead of marginal prices, and this has been explicitly mentioned in describing the following studies.

8   ELECTRICAL SUPPLY AND DEMAND

FIGURE 1.2

Price-Quantity Relationship with Inelastic Demand
for Electricity

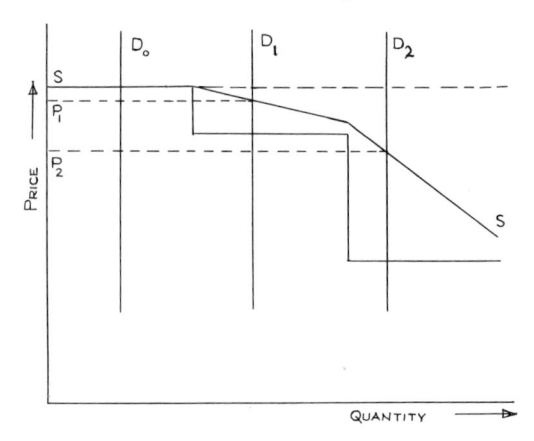

Source: Compiled by the author.

One of the earliest studies carried out in this field, and one that is extensively quoted, was authored by Franklin M. Fisher and Carl Kaysen.[1] This study analyzed the demand for electricity in the household as well as in the industrial sector. Although Fisher and Kaysen have emphasized and dealt with the econometric problems involved in estimation of electricity demand, a lack of proper data reduced the strength of their conclusions. Their study has been described in some detail in this book mainly because of its prominence in the field and the frequent references made to it in the literature since its publication.

Household behavior has been viewed by Fisher and Kaysen as consisting of two parts—that which deals with the intensity of use of a given stock of appliances, that is, the short run; and that which deals with the stock of appliances itself, that is, the long run. Thus, they have attempted to estimate the short run determinants of demand, given a stock of "white goods," or appliances, on the one hand, and the determinants of white goods stocks on the other.

Using a microeconomic model of the use of household appliances, Fisher and Kaysen's short run demand equation is derived as

$$D'_t = A' + \alpha P'_t + \beta Y'_t + W'_t + u_t$$

where the primes denote logarithms and the subscript t denotes the relevant time period. Therefore,

$D_t \equiv$ demand for electricity by all households in the community;

$P_t \equiv$ average price of electricity;

$Y_t \equiv$ per capita personal income;

$W_t \equiv$ the aggregate of white goods in the community;

$u \equiv$ a disturbance term; and

A, α, and β are constant parameters.

The authors then estimated this model by taking first differences between successive time periods. This enabled them to overcome the difficulties inherent in collecting data for household appliances and aggregating them in terms of a common unit, because the term for stock of appliances was eliminated by taking first differences. The first differenced equation would then be of the form

$$\Delta D'_t = \alpha \Delta P'_t + \beta \Delta Y'_t + \Delta W'_t + u_t$$

Fisher and Kaysen then assumed that $\Delta W'_t$ was a constant; or, in other words, the rate of growth of the stock of appliances was a constant for the community. To get estimates of the coefficients in this model, they used data for the period 1946-57 for 47 different states (North and South Carolina being considered as one unit, as also Maryland the the District of Columbia, respectively). Although Fisher and Kaysen mention that the size and composition of the stock of white goods in year t should be expected to be influenced by an average of past incomes and of past prices, their model explicitly uses current incomes and prices only. This is predicated on the assumption that the current incomes and prices would tend to be correlated highly with moving averages of their respective past values. Perhaps this assumption is valid when applied to data for the period 1946-57, but it can hardly be expected to hold in the future with the unexpected movements and reversals in trends that are forecast.

Further, Fisher and Kaysen used real price of electricity as the price variable; they state that the correlation between money price and real price, which must exist in a time series, would be eliminated by taking first differences. Thus the identification problem posed by a declining rate schedule (as explained earlier in conjunction with Figures 1.1 and 1.2) will also be negligible because they assume a negligible shift in the real price schedule facing the consumer over time. This is stated by them as, "Over time, the rate schedule relationship between the real price of electricity and the amount of electricity used can be expected to be almost non-existent, whatever is the case for the relationship with money price. This is so because the rate schedules tend to remain fairly constant while the price index shifts through time."[2] Again, this observation may have been true for the period 1946-57, but certainly rate schedules have not been constant in the 1970s, which would introduce a serious error in results obtained with the Fisher and Kaysen model if applied to that data, and even more so if used for future forecasts.

The results of the Fisher and Kaysen study indicated overall that price and income were not significant in the demand relationship. On the basis of the nature of their results for the 47 states, Fisher and Kaysen predicted that the significance of price would decrease and that of income increase in the future. Robert Halvorsen[3] used their model for the period 1961-69 and found no validity in their predictions.

In estimating long run demand for electricity, Fisher and Kaysen attempt to study the determinants of the stock of appliances in the long run. The model used by them pertaining to the ith type of appliances is

$$W'_{it} - W'_{it-1} = A_i + \eta_{i1}(Y^{E'}_t - Y^{E'}_{t-1}) + \eta_{i2}Y'_t + \eta_{i3}E'_{it}$$
$$+ (\eta_{i4}G'_{it}) + \eta_{i5}(H'_t - H'_{t-1}) + \eta_{i6}(F'_t - F'_{t-1})$$
$$+ \eta_{i7}M'_t + \eta_{i8}P^{E'}_t + \eta_{i9}\gamma'_{it} + (\eta_{i10}V^{E'}_t) + U_{it}$$

where again the primes indicate logarithms, t the time period, and

- W ≡ a stock of appliances or "white goods,"
- A ≡ a constant term,
- η_{ij} ≡ a series of coefficients to be estimated,
- Y^E ≡ a moving average of real personal income per capita,
- Y ≡ real personal income per capita for the period,
- E ≡ price of the white good concerned,
- G ≡ price of the gas-using substitute (if any),
- H ≡ number of electricity customers per capita,
- F ≡ population,
- M ≡ number of marriages during the period,
- P^E ≡ expected real price of electricity (measured by means of a three-year moving average),

$\gamma \equiv$ KwH consumption of a new unit of the appliance per hour of average use,

$V^E \equiv$ a three-year moving average of gas prices, and

$U \equiv$ a random error term.

The authors term this formulation an "infectious disease" model—the infectiousness of the disease to buy appliances being influenced by all the independent variables in the model. This model does not differentiate between the degrees of saturation reached in the stocks of a particular appliance. The authors admit, "We have made no provision for the fact that the disease cannot spread very fast in percentage terms when nearly everybody has got it."[4]

The data available to the authors for application of their model were, by their own admission, inadequate. Thus, they had to carry out various approximations to construct appropriate time series for seven different types of appliances, but the results for three were not presented because of various deficiencies. On the basis of the estimates obtained by them, Fisher and Kaysen concluded that the price of electricity as well as the price of appliances do not have substantial effects on the stock of appliances. The major determinants of appliance stocks were found to be changes in long run incomes, in population, and in the number of wired households per capita.

At a glance it can be seen that the variables found to be significant by Fisher and Kaysen are precisely those whose first differences have been included in the right-hand side of the demand model above. The left-hand side in this model is also a first difference of logarithms of appliance stocks. All the other dependent variables included are not in the form of first differences but single period levels. This is apparently the cause of the insignificance of these variables in the Fisher and Kaysen estimates. As an analogy one could view this discrepancy as being similar to a consumption function specified with a flow variable on the left-hand side and only stock variables such as wealth on the right-hand side. Clearly, a complete specification for consumption should include changes in wealth (or income) as an independent variable also. Thus, the long run model of residential demand has not only deficiencies in data for estimation but some conceptual flaws as well. Hence, the Fisher and Kaysen model is inappropriate for application to long range forecasting, particularly with the reversal in price trends occurring since 1974.

The Fisher and Kaysen industrial demand model rests on the assumption that electricity is an input in the production of industrial goods and has two components—one fixed and the other variable. The fixed part consists of lighting and heating functions, which do not vary with the size of the output for all practical purposes. The variable part of course consists of uses such as running machines and feeding certain electrochemical processes, which naturally vary with the rate of activity or output of the plant. Then for the ith industrial establishment

$$D_{it} = A_i + B_i X_{it} + U_{it}$$

where $D_{it} \equiv$ total electricity used by the plant, $X_{it} \equiv$ the output of the plant, A_i and B_i are constant parameters and U_{it} is a random disturbance term. Since the price of electricity would have an influence on output (the firm would always vary output such that marginal cost equals marginal revenue), the above model was modified as

$$D_{it} = A_i + B_i X_{it} P_{it}^{\pi_i} + U_{it}$$

where $P_{it} \equiv$ the real price of electricity to the firm and π_i is a parameter, other terms being as before. The authors had various problems using this model with available data. For one thing, for all industries in a two-digit group, prices of electricity used by them in different states would be different. Unfortunately industrial data were only available by two-digit Standard Industrial Classification (SIC) codes, and thus a nationwide weighted average of prices was required for use in the model. Data were used for 10 different industry groups; and, on the assumption of constant technology within each group, the above model was modified by using the approximation

$$D_{It} = K X_{It}^{\beta} P_{It}^{\alpha} + V_{It}$$

the suffix I standing for a particular industry group. The model was used in logarithmic form to obtain least-squares estimates, output being measured in terms of value added by manufacture to aggregate outputs of different types of goods.

The results obtained by Fisher and Kaysen indicated a significant negative price effect in six of the ten industry groups and a nonsignificant negative price effect in two more. Further, the value of the price effect showed elasticity greater than unity in six cases, but it was stated that the authors perhaps had overestimated elasticity on account of locational effects inherent in such an analysis. In other words, industries would locate in regions with low prices of electricity if they used relatively greater amounts of electric power. However in estimates based on cross-sectional data, this locational effect also would be included in the differences in output observed in relation to prices.

EXISTING STUDIES AND MODELS

To that extent the estimate of response to price changes would be exaggerated.

The second part of the industrial sector study by Fisher and Kaysen deals with trying to evaluate the extent of technological change in each industry group. Their aim was to investigate whether there was any change in magnitude and direction in the electric input coefficient for different industries. Lack of adequate data limited this investigation of change to an analysis of the electricity input coefficients for different industries in 1947 and 1956. The ratios of these coefficients for 1956 to those for 1947 were then ranked in descending order alongside a column of cost ratios, respectively, for each industry group. From a ranking of these two columns the authors drew certain inferences on the type of change that had taken place from 1947 to 1956. The picture available from this necessarily was crude, since even the cost ratios computed and ranked by the authors were the ratio of total electricity cost to value of shipments. The value of shipments during any time period is by no means an accurate indicator of total output during that period, though often it is used in the absence of more precise data.

It must be stated that although Fisher and Kaysen were hampered in their study by a lack of adequate data, they were able to lay a cogent framework for analysis of industrial demand for electricity. This undoubtedly helped other researchers in their studies.

An exhaustive study of residential and industrial demand for electricity was also carried out by John W. Wilson.[5] His work in the section pertaining to residential demand consists of (1) an extended critique of previous studies, particularly the Fisher and Kaysen study described earlier; (2) an analysis of the determinants of the quantity of electricity demanded by the household; and (3) an analysis of the demand for selected major residential electric appliances.

Wilson referred to the problem discussed at the beginning of this chapter, namely, that of accounting for the effect of quantity consumed on price of electricity. However, his estimation technique did not include a simultaneous specification of the supply schedule, which in real life makes price an endogenously determined value. The author reasoned that to approximate marginal price effects, the alternative specification using typical electric bill (TEB)[*] values in addition to average price largely corrected the bias that would be inherent in

---

[*] TEB, or typical electric bills, are published annually by the Federal Power Commission, Washington, D.C., and provide data on average prices of electricity in units of 500, 1,000, 1,500 KwH, and so on. Data for beginning and end of year bills are averaged to correct for seasonally varying differences within a year.

the use of average price only. He estimated the demand equation in a number of different forms, of which the log-linear using TEB data was apparently the most plausible and conclusive. In all the different formulations a significant negative price-quantity relationship was obtained, and the values of elasticity were found to be greater than unity in every case.

However, the income coefficient in the demand equation, obtained in each of the different formulations, was significantly negative. It is strange that this apparent paradox was not investigated by Wilson, and stranger still that in the extensive discussions of the regression results, meager mention has been made of the negative income elasticity estimates obtained by him.

Wilson's residential demand study included an analysis of demand for different electrical appliances as well. The independent variables used in the appliance model are the same as for the quantity of electricity—namely, price of electricity, price of gas, income, climate variable, and so on. Again, both average price of electricity and TEB data were used in the estimation procedure, which covered the demands for ranges, water heaters, clothes dryers, space heaters, food freezers, and air conditioners. Some of the results obtained are of interest. For instance, electric heating is used more in areas with mild climates than in colder regions. Price of electricity was again found to be a significant determinant of demand for all the appliances, except air conditioners. Income elasticities in some of these cases, too, were negative, implying that such appliances are inferior goods. The stock of electric dryers is negatively correlated with warm climates and positively with income, which is a plausible conclusion. The appliance demand study by Wilson does have certain improvements over the Fisher and Kaysen study on account of the use of census figures by the former as against sales figures obtained by the latter from a trade publication. Further, stocks of appliances are in terms of percentage of homes equipped with them rather than absolute values, which makes this quantity more meaningful in aggregating data in an econometric study.

Wilson also carried out a study of demand in the industrial sector. This included estimation of the coefficients in the model for general industrial demand for electric power, internal or self-generated electricity being accounted for in the quantity of alternative sources used such as gas, coal, and oil. It also included an analysis of demand in certain specific two-digit SIC industry groups. The unit of demand was specified as kilowatt hour/value added to make comparisons possible between different industries exhibiting differences in absolute size, as well as within the same industry group for different regional locations.

The specification of the demand equations included independent variables representing (1) prices of alternative energy sources such as gas, coal, and fuel oil; (2) the metropolitan area's rate of industrial growth (value added in 1963/value added in 1954), and (3) a proxy for the capital intensity of production techniques [1 - salaries and wages/value added]. The rationale for including prices of alternative energy sources is in the fact that the closest substitutes to commercially available electricity would not only be these alternative fuels themselves but the generation of internally produced electricity, for which costs would be determined largely by the prices of alternative fuels used for power generation. A number of regressions were carried out by the author, employing different forms of the demand equation. The best results were obtained when relative prices of coal with respect to commercially available electricity and for fuel oil with respect to electricity were used. The author explained the fact that cross-price elasticities using these price ratios included not only the direct effects of changes in price ratios on an established industry but the effect of such differences in price ratios on the locational decisions of industries as well. Since the study has used cross-sectional data, on the assumption that differences in the cross section reflect similar differences over a period of time, there is every reason to believe that those industries that use relatively large proportions of electricity in their production processes would locate in regions exhibiting lower prices of electricity. This hypothesis is defended by the author in an extended discussion wherein some computed values for the entire nation and the Tennessee Valley Authority (TVA) region (which had lower electricity prices than most of the rest of the United States) are presented. The comparison is made by

(1) computing actual value added by industry groups for the TVA region by two-digit SIC groups;
(2) computing similar values using national data by three- or four-digit SIC groups;
(3) aggregating electricity consumption by three- or four-digit SIC groups for the whole nation;
(4) arriving at the ratio of kilowatt hour/value added for each industry group for the United States, using values computed in (2) and (3); and
(5) multiplying the value of kilowatt hour/value added in (4) by the actual value added in each industry group for the TVA region.

The value obtained in (5) provides a theoretical base for electricity consumption, which is compared with the actual consumption. If the former is lower, it could be concluded that electricity consumption in such industries is probably higher because the kilowatt hour/

value added for industry subgroups within an industry group is higher. In other words, the industry mix is such that those industries that are relatively electricity-intensive have located in the cheaper electricity region. A number of other computations were presented to advocate the contention of a locational effect. Unfortunately, the statistical strength of such a conclusion could only be overwhelming if it were possible to hold a number of controlled experiments to observe the effects of electricity price on industry location. However, with the limited nature of data available, the author has been able to substantiate to some extent a contention which, in any case, seems valid on self-evident grounds.

Another cross-sectional analysis of residential demand for electricity was carried out by Kent P. Anderson.[6] In that study the author estimated models of residential demand both for the United States as a whole and the state of California. In his specification of the demand equation Anderson assumed that a certain fraction, δ, of the customers in the year $t-1$ would remain "locked-in" to their stock of appliances and electricity use in the year t. Demand would then be given by

$$D = \delta D_{-1} + F(\cdot)(H - \delta H_{-1})$$

where $D \equiv$ residential demand for electricity, $F(\cdot) \equiv$ a function determining average demand per flexible customer, and $H \equiv$ number of customer households. The subscript, -1, stands for values for the previous year. For estimation purposes Anderson also used a supply equation, thereby avoiding the typical identification problem encountered in electricity demand studies. The above demand equation was used to provide an expression for $F(\cdot)$, which is

$$F(\cdot) = \frac{D - \delta D_{-1}}{H - \delta H_{-1}}$$

This was then estimated by ordinary least-squares (OLS), using data for 1968 and 1969 with an equation of the form

$$\ln DE = a_0 + a_1 \cdot \ln DCE + a_2 \cdot \ln PG + a_3 \cdot \ln RYPH + a_4 \cdot \ln SOH$$
$$+ a_5 \cdot NMP + a_6 \cdot WTEMP + a_7 \cdot STEMP + u$$

where

$DE \equiv$ the function $F(\cdot)$ defined earlier,

$CE \equiv$ average real cost to residential customers of 500 KwH per month,

DCE ≡ average real cost to residential customers of 1,000 KwH per month - CE,

PG ≡ average real cost of gas to residential customers,

RYPH ≡ average real personal income per household,

SOH ≡ average size of household,

NMP ≡ fraction of population living in nonmetropolitan areas,

WTEMP ≡ average January temperature,

STEMP ≡ average July temperature,

u ≡ a random error term, and

a_0-a_7 ≡ coefficients to be estimated.

This general equation was estimated using alternative assumptions for δ included in the dependent variable DE. The electricity price variables used TEB data both for DCE and CE. Hence it can be seen that Anderson's estimation used a reduced form equation of the demand and supply functions. The actual estimates obtained by the author showed stability over a wide range of values assumed for δ. He, therefore, concluded that this could be only the result of a steady growth of residential demand and customer households in the years leading up to 1969. Anderson also correctly argued that since, with steady growth in demand and customer households, only the constant term would be affected with different values of δ, cross-sectional estimates for a fixed point in time can be taken as indicative of true long run behavior.

The estimates obtained by Anderson for 1969 cross-sectional data were -0.91 for own price elasticity and 1.13 for income elasticity of residential electricity demand. These differed significantly from Wilson's estimates, a large part of the variation being accounted for perhaps by the fact that whereas Anderson used data for all 50 states, Wilson's estimates were based on data for 77 major cities only. But again the lack of a 'dynamic response of demand to changes in prices and incomes renders Anderson's model unsuitable for long run forecasts, particularly when applied to a period of time characterized by trend changes in prices and incomes.

Another interesting study has been authored by T. J. Tyrrell for the Oak Ridge National Laboratory.[7] The model specified by him formulates total demand for electricity as a function of population, per capita personal income, the price of electricity, the prices of competing energy sources, and the prices of electrical appliances. The model is estimated by OLS in logarithmic form and assumes variable elasticities. In other words, the implication is that residential customers are more sensitive to price changes when prices are relatively high. The lag in response is also assumed to be variable and geometric in form. Thus the estimates yield a dynamic pattern of adjustment of demand to changes in the independent variables. The elasticity estimates related to price of electricity are greater than unity both in the long run and short run, with 1971 average residential price as the base.

Further, Tyrrell made projections up to the year 2000 and tested the model for sensitivity, highlighting the extent of variation in demand projections for different assumptions regarding prices, per capita income, and population. Per capita income and price of electricity yield the largest percentage variation of demand in response to different income and electricity price variations.

By far the most exhaustive and thorough investigation made thus far into the determinants of demand for electricity, particularly in the residential sector, has been carried out by Halvorsen.[8] The residential demand study for the long run[9] and the short run[10] is based on the author's doctoral dissertation work at Harvard.[11] However, the main findings of his doctoral research are presented lucidly in the two reports mentioned above. The long run demand study is based on a number of alternative assumptions and formulations. To allow for the identification problem described earlier, Halvorsen found it necessary to specify a general demand as well as general supply model.

The general form of the demand equation specified is

$$Q = Q(P, Y, \underline{W}, u)$$

where Q is quantity demanded in kilowatt hours, P is the marginal electricity price, Y is income, $\underline{W}$ is the vector of all other relevant variables, and u is a disturbance term. The general form of the price equation is

$$P = P(Q, \underline{X}, v)$$

where P and Q are as before, $\underline{X}$ is a vector of the exogenous factors affecting the price schedule, and v is a disturbance term.

These two are the structural equations of the model, but elimination of the price variable in the two would yield a combined reduced form equation. Elasticities of demand calculated from the structural equations, referred to as direct elasticities, represent the extent of movement of the demand curve; but elasticities calculated from the reduced form equation would represent not only the resultant movement of the demand curve but also along the price schedule. This is because of the dependence of price on the quantity consumed. In other words, the total elasticity of demand with respect to electricity price

EXISTING STUDIES AND MODELS 19

measures the total effect on demand of a parallel shift in the price schedule (see Fig. 1.1).

The paucity of data for marginal price was overcome by estimating the structural equations using average price data. Once this is done, estimates are obtained for the average price equation; and, using the relationship between average and marginal price, the marginal price equation is estimated. The demand equation is again estimated using marginal price by substituting in the originally estimated demand equation the value of average price (Pa) in terms of marginal price (Pm). $P_a = P_m/(1 + e)$ is the average price relationship used for this purpose, where e is the elasticity of supply.

Halvorsen also contends that on theoretical grounds, undoubtedly, marginal price is the relevant decision variable; but in actual life information costs to the consumer are so high that he does not compute a comparison of marginal cost against the marginal benefits of each extra unit consumed by him. On the other hand, most consumers are generally aware of their monthly electric bills and presumably of the total quantities consumed by them. As such, average price would be a relevant variable to use in the demand model. The author found that estimates based on average price did not yield values any different from those based on marginal price.

The reduced form equation is also estimated from estimates of the structural equations, and this yielded values of total elasticity of demand. Additionally, the reduced form equation is estimated using TEB data as a proxy for the price schedule. This provided the author with a broad check of the estimates obtained from the structural equations.

Since the response of demand to changes in prices and other variables is likely to be in the nature of a lagged effect, the author estimated the demand equations with assumptions of different lag structures including a five-year simple average, nine-year simple average, five-year inverted V, nine-year inverted V, and first- and second-order Pascal lag. Estimation of these models was carried out using data for the 48 contiguous states in the United States for the years 1961-69. Also a static model was estimated using pooled data. The results of the regression showed that the choice of the model had little or no effect on the estimates. In fact the static model gave almost identical estimates to those obtained for the dynamic formulations. This is perhaps on account of the fact that during 1961-69 prices of electricity followed a generally similar downward trend countrywide, and as such a cross section at any time during this period was representative of the pattern of differences running over the entire period. The formulation of the structural demand equation used by Halvorsen is reproduced below.

$$Q = Q(P_a, Y, G, A, D, J, R, M, H, T, u)$$

where

$Q \equiv$ average annual electricity sales per customer,

$P_a \equiv$ average real price of residential electricity,

$Y \equiv$ average real income per capita,

$G \equiv$ average real price per therm for all types of gas,

$A \equiv$ index of real wholesale prices of electric equipment,

$D \equiv$ heating degree days,

$J \equiv$ average July temperature,

$R \equiv$ percentage of population living in rural areas,

$M \equiv$ percentage of housing units in multiunit structures,

$H \equiv$ average size of households,

$T \equiv$ time, and

$u \equiv$ disturbance term.

Halvorsen omitted fuel oil as an independent variable due to lack of data and mentions that this omission is likely to have biased the coefficients of income and gas price away from zero. It would be reasonable to assume that the main impact of this would perhaps be on the gas price coefficient since fuel oil and gas price probably have maintained a constant ratio over time. Thus we may conclude that Halvorsen's long run gas price elasticity is to a large extent an estimate for combined gas plus fuel oil elasticity. However, according to the author, it is possible that because of the fact that gas has become available in certain states only recently and due to possible long lags in response of demand, the estimates of gas price elasticity obtained by him are biased toward zero. The author's own price elasticity for electricity demand, however, was found to be significantly greater than unity with all the models and the income elasticity significantly less than unity.

In the most recent publication by Halvorsen,[12] he also estimated models for demand in the commercial and industrial sectors. These are based on static models in both cases, since the residential demand model had exhibited little variation in the estimates obtained between the static and dynamic formulations. The price elasticity in the commercial sector was found to be somewhat higher than unity and in the industrial sector substantially greater than unity. Again estimation is carried out using price equations in each case, with both TEB data as well as a price function using cost variables.

Halvorsen's work brings out the importance of prices of electricity as well as those of substitutes in the aggregate demand for electricity. The pricing policies with regard to these sources of energy must therefore be formulated in the future with this evidence in mind. Prices, according to the author, can be used as useful rationing mechanisms.

The literature surveyed above pertains to econometric studies of demand for electricity. A systems dynamics study in this field was carried out by the Battelle Memorial Institute[13] in modeling the activities within the Susquehanna River Basin. However, this study did not specifically identify the data used and statistical applications thereof. The "power-requirements" sector in that model includes

(1) per household consumption of electricity exclusive of heating (this component has been specified to grow exponentially in the model);

(2) average household consumption for heating, which is a function of per household consumption for heating and the fraction of the total households using electric heating (the per household consumption figure is assumed to remain constant over time, and the fraction variable grows linearly at an assumed rate);

(3) per household serving worker consumption of electricity, which also grows exponentially over time; and

(4) an industrial sector in which consumption per industrial worker grows exponentially over time.

Each of these per unit consumption values is multiplied by the relevant population or level existing during a particular time interval to determine total power requirements. This model has neither the economic basis nor the degree of detail necessary to give it plausibility and responsiveness to changes in other activities. Hence, at best, it can be called a trend extrapolation model for electricity "requirements."

NOTES

1. Franklin M. Fisher and Carl Kaysen, <u>A Study in Econometrics, The Demand for Electricity in the United States</u> (Amsterdam, Holland: North Holland Publishing Company, 1962).

2. Ibid.

3. Robert Halvorsen, <u>Short-Run Determinants of Residential Electricity Demand</u>, Discussion Paper 73-10 (Seattle: Institute for Economic Research, 1973).

4. Fisher and Kaysen, op. cit.

5. John W. Wilson, Residential and Industrial Demand for Electricity: An Emprical Analysis (Ann Arbor, Mich.: University Microfilms, Inc., 1969).

6. Kent P. Anderson, Residential Demand for Electricity: Econometric Estimates for California and the United States (Santa Monica, Calif.: The Rand Corporation, 1972).

7. "Tennessee Valley Authority," Forbes (April 1, 1975).

8. Robert Halvorsen, Demand for Electric Power in the United States, Discussion Paper 13-13 (Seattle: Institute for Economic Research, 1973).

9. Robert Halvorsen, Long-Run Residential Demand for Electricity, Discussion Paper 73-6 (Seattle: Institute for Economic Research, 1973).

10. Halvorsen, Short-Run Determinants of Residential Electricity Demand, op. cit.

11. Robert Halvorsen, Residential Demand for Electricity (Cambridge, Mass.: Environmental Systems Program, 1972).

12. Halvorsen, Demand for Electric Power in the United States, op. cit.

13. Battelle Memorial Institute, A Dynamic Model of the Economy of the Susquehanna River Basin (Washington: Battelle Memorial Institute, 1966).

CHAPTER

2

DEVELOPMENT OF A SUITABLE FORECASTING METHODOLOGY

THE SYSTEMS DYNAMICS CONCEPT

The systems dynamics simulation technique was established by Jay W. Forrester of Massachusetts Institute of Technology and developed as described in his book Industrial Dynamics.[1] The concept was designed to provide an easy vehicle for management and policy makers to enable a study of the effects of policy changes in an industrial system. This was achieved by constructing a model of the company's policy-making actions, information flow, production, and distribution activities. With the use of a computer this model was allowed to run under certain policy assumptions—both overt and implicit—and simulations carried out to represent a desired time span. Thus, the policy maker was able to test the full effect of his policies on different parts of the total system, without subjecting the organization to the consequences of those policies in real life. The underlying theory behind systems dynamics (as it is now called in its broader connotations) is to treat all activities in a system in terms of levels and flows. This concept is not foreign to economic theory and application, wherein economic variables also represent either stocks or flows. In fact, a differentiation between stock and flow concepts in economics is essential to the proper understanding of an economic system.

Forrester visualized the application of systems dynamics to economic activity, but this was foreseen in the same framework as for engineering systems. The emphasis in such models was to afford greater reliance on descriptive information than on measurement. "In formulating a model of a system, we should rely less exclusively on statistics and formal data and make better use of our vast store of descriptive information."[2] Such an approach would perhaps explain adequately the behavior of a system but cannot be expected to yield a precise quantitative prediction of variables characterizing its activities.

This book attempts to bridge the gap between a truly prediction-oriented study and one that only brings out some of the behavioral characteristics of the components of the system. Most econometric models often suppress the feedback effects and dynamic variations inherent in any economic system; this happens because such models either embody static single-period relationships or only pick up composite trends pertinent to the particular time span considered at the time of formulation. Static relationships when abstracted from their dynamic effects can be misleading. An early illustration of this was furnished in the late 1930s by Paul Samuelson.[3] In this particular study, he constructed a simple model in which he assumed that for any unit time interval (1) government deficit spending is $1; (2) marginal propensity to consume is one-half (that is, consumption in any period is equal to one-half the national income of the previous period); and (3) induced private investment is proportional to the increase in consumption between the previous and the current period. Samuelson then exhibits that with this simple model starting in any period, the values of consumption and investment follow a series of fluctuations that get explosive over a period of time. This phenomenon has been studied further in the literature on difference equations. However, most models based on difference equations have been explored in the literature by arriving at a solution of the equations in the system and studying the characteristics of the roots. This typically involves the computation of values of variables being investigated for a succession of time intervals. Essentially the same result is achieved by systems dynamics simulations, but the use of a computer eliminates the need for a study of the roots themselves and at the same time facilitates the modeling of a much more complex system consisting of an unlimited number of equations. It is important that in arriving at forecasts of electrical energy demand an understanding be gained also of the mechanism by which such demand is generated and of the behavior of the economic-demographic system involved. This book is concerned not only with evolving a suitable methodology for forecasting demand but also investigating the nature of the system that generates demand to develop policy alternatives in relation to supply.

The unit time interval used in this simulation is two months. There are three reasons for the selection of this value.

(1) A large unit time interval such as a year largely would have obscured some of the dynamic variations that are obtainable with a shorter time interval. (Hereafter, the time interval will be referred to as DT.)

FORECASTING METHODOLOGY 25

(2) By adopting a large DT it would not be possible to build seasonal variations in demand for electricity. Although seasonal factors have not been regarded as very important in the past, they are a major factor in deciding a utility's generating capacity. However, seasonality effects have been considered only later in this book to develop specific policies.

(3) A smaller DT of, say, one month perhaps would have been preferable, but the marginal advantages from such finer sensitivity would be outweighed by the higher costs of computation involved in doubling the number of iterations for a given time horizon.

The simulations conducted with this model make use of the FORTRAN WATFIV computer language, and the essential features as well as subroutines employed are similar to those formulated by R. W. Llewellyn in his book FORDYN.[4] The model has been initiallized with the values pertaining to mid-1968, and values for 134 subsequent time intervals have been obtained by simulation. Thus, the time span covered by the study extends from mid-1968 to the end of 1990, with values of selected variables tabulated and plotted for each bimonthly interval, by means of Llewellyn's OUTPC and PLOTC subroutines.

The basis on which each model equation has been specified and the methods by which estimates of coefficients have been obtained are detailed in the subsequent sections. The general format of the model, however, consists of a residential sector, an industrial sector, and a commercial sector. The dependent variable in each equation determines whether that equation represents a level, flow, or auxiliary variable. The assumption used in systems dynamics is that if a sufficiently small DT is adopted, the values only at the start of a time interval determine the flow rates during that interval. Hence, during the interval DT flow rates remain constant, but add to or subtract from the values of levels and auxiliary variables to yield a new set of values for the latter. This concept is similar to approximating a continuous curve by a series of discrete steps equal to the mean values of the curve for each particular interval: the smaller the step (or DT in our case), the closer the approximation to the true continuous curve.

Systems dynamics has been applied to a variety of social systems, most notably the models described by Forrester in Urban Dynamics[5] and World Dynamics.[6] These models, however, contain a serious flaw. The emphasis on descriptive knowledge, unsupported by empirical evidence, renders these models susceptible to subjective bias and theoretical inconsistencies. Systems dynamics therefore has become anathema to economists and those who believe in the law that theory should be supported by empirical evidence. The criticism against Forrester's technique has been brought out with substantial validity in an article by William D. Nordhaus.[7] The author contends, in reference to Forrester's World Dynamics, that "the treatment of empirical relations in World Dynamics can be summarized as measurement without data." Nordhaus notes in detail some of the theoretical flaws in Forrester's model and concludes, "World Dynamics contains no clear concepts of production functions, consumption, or output; nor is there any discernible method of allocating resources over time or between sectors." Going a step further, Nordhaus used Forrester's model and carried out simulations of his own, using a set of underlying assumptions different from Forrester's. He found that "the predictions of the world's future are highly sensitive to the specification of the model. Simulations given above indicate that if assumptions regarding population, technological chage, or substitution are changed, Forrester's model behaves in a dramatically different manner."

Two aspects of Nordhaus' criticism have been taken into account in the model used for developing the subject matter in this book.

(1) The model equations have been estimated strictly on the basis of relevant data. Some parameters, such as measures of different price and income elasticities, have been extracted from other published works and studies, which are well founded on good empirical evidence.

(2) Realizing the uncertainties inherent in any economic forecast today, a large number of simulations have been carried out to test the results in response to a series of changes in assumptions. This is designed not only to provide a range of forecasts or probable outcomes on which the utility bases its investment decisions but also to arrive at a plausible range of values within which the interaction between supply and demand will occur in the future.

In concluding this discussion on systems dynamics it would be appropriate to emphasize that this technique presents a powerful potential for application to economic systems. At the same time it is essential to recognize that model building of this type must be supported as much as possible by actual data and statistical techniques. Whenever actual measurement is not altogether possible, coefficients and parameters could perhaps be adopted as the result of simulations themselves. For instance the structure and magnitude of lags in the economy often are not measurable without certain assumptions being made in the specification of the model. By means of simulations, one could use a variety of reasonable assumptions and select the one that appears to provide results most suitable in explaining the behavior and state of the system.

With greater awareness of the consequences of economic policy making, most governments could use macroeconomic models of complex economic systems profitably to pretest the effects of bold measures by means of systems dynamics simulations, instead of actually implementing them in practice and bearing the cost of probable failure. Later chapters in this book describe how the basic model used herein could explain policy making by the individual utility concerned and also the manner in which its implications can be enlarged to apply to the future supply and demand of electrical energy in the entire United States.

MODEL SPECIFICATION

In specifying the model in this study, it was found necessary at every stage to keep the characteristics of the particular system being modeled in perspective. However, although the entire structure and form of the model has been designed for the specific region served by Carolina Power and Light, it can be transformed to suit the characteristics of any other geographic entity if so desired. Activity in the system has been divided into three separate sectors, namely, residential or domestic, industrial, and commercial. This classification is generally followed by most utilities in the nation, and their rate structures are also consistent with this particular division or grouping of different customers. Certain peripheral services provided by the utility have not been included in the model, since they amount to less than 1 percent of total sales, for example, highway lighting, which is sold as a complete package by the utility modeled and includes provision for maintenance and replenishment of consumable supplies on highway lighting equipment. Further, it has been assumed that the growth of demand for electricity not sold directly by Carolina Power and Light but resold by cooperatives and municipal agencies would follow the same path, proportionally, as the rest of the system.

RESIDENTIAL SECTOR

The residential sector consists of three separate rate groups, which, for the purposes of this study, have been designated as

(1) high consumption rate group—including households living in all-electric homes or separately metered apartments;

(2) medium consumption rate group—consisting of households using a company-approved water heater installed in the home; and
(3) low consumption rate group—consisting of any household that is a customer of the electric utility.

The proportion of customers in each of the rate groups has been changing over a period of time, as has the total number of customer households in all the groups. The fraction of customers assigned to each group in this study has been determined by a set of relationships estimated from data provided by the North Carolina Utilities Commission. The specification of these equations used the percentage of customers in a particular rate group as the dependent variable, and average kilowatt hours per customer and a time trend as independent variables. These were also specified in certain alternative forms and estimated as described in the next section. It would perhaps have been most logical to treat each rate group as a more or less homogeneous population and compute demand for electricity as a function of economic variables specific to each group. This was not possible for two reasons.

First, contrary to what one may expect, customers in each rate group exhibit considerable disparities in economic status. For instance one may expect a strong correlation between electricity consumption and household income, but it was found on the basis of available information that a large number of low income houses were all electric, whereas a large proportion of high income households used gas and home heating oil for water heating and space heating. This is not to say that the income elasticity of demand for electricity is close to zero or negative, but apparently the response of demand to price and income changes is a continuous process. There is no such thing as a steady state in the types and degrees of electricity use in the household.

Second, data are not available for income characteristics of each rate group. Whatever information was available could be gleaned only on the basis of discussions with North Carolina state and utility officials, since no formal survey of the economic status of customers was carried out by the utility. The 1970 census contains information that could be applied to this area; but these figures do not correspond separately to the utility's individual rate groups and, in any case, are not directly applicable to the specific geographic area served by any utility.

An electricity demand model can be expected to be highly sensitive to population changes, and hence the computation of reliable population estimates is essential in a dynamic model. Population changes are caused by (1) births, (2) deaths, and (3) migration. Birth rates and migration have been estimated by a set of OLS regressions and death rates by merely extrapolating the trends observed from past data for reasons to be explained later. It would have been preferable to break down the total population of the region by different age groups. The original specification of the model included three age groups— zero to 18 years, 18 to 65 years, and 65 and over. This was done in view of the fact that not only is the birth rate normally determined by the existing population in the lower age groups (which have higher fertility rates), but the age structure gives a better measure of demand in the society for such age-specific uses as schools and recreational facilities. However, to determine any set of equations involving these different age groups, it would be necessary to use time series data for estimation. Such data do not exist, nor was it possible to obtain time series for the age structure of migrants into or out of the region. Thus the specification of population by age groups had to be abandoned, and only a measure for total population was retained in the model.

Having determined the total population of the region for a particular time interval, it is then necessary to determine the total number of households. Average size of household was observed to be decreasing steadily over a period of time; and the rate of change for every DT was estimated by extrapolation on the basis of a steady past trend which, it was assumed, will continue up to 1990, the terminal point of this forecast. Thus, the total number of households is estimated based on a computation of total population and average size of households. This, in turn, is used to determine the number of households (or residential customers) in each rate group, since the percentage in each rate group is known, as described earlier.

A critical part in the residential sector involves the microeconomic analysis of electricity demand by the household. The factors bringing about changes in electricity demand would be changes in (1) real price of electricity, (2) real price of gas and home heating oil, (3) real income per capita, and (4) a time trend that would include the effects of introduction of new appliances. The studies reviewed earlier included a large number of variables as determinants of residential demand. Some of these were average July temperature, heating degree days, and average size of households. The first two were not considered in this model since they can be expected to remain fairly stable in the same region; and the third, although not found to be very important by Halvorsen in his estimates,[8] is included in this study for determining the total number of residential customers and hence is a determinant of total residential demand.

Estimates of elasticities of demand with respect to electricity price, price of gas, and income are available from the studies discussed earlier. No formal estimates of elasticities for home heating oil were available in the literature, nor were adequate data available for a proper estimation of this parameter. However, there is reason to believe that

30   ELECTRICITY SUPPLY AND DEMAND

FIGURE 2.1

Structure of Lagged Effects of Prices and Incomes

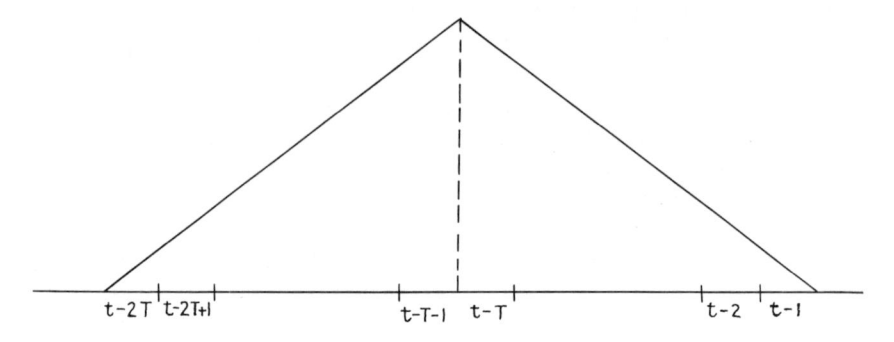

[figure: triangular lag structure with x-axis markers t-2T, t-2T+1, ..., t-T-1, t-T, ..., t-2, t-1]

Source: Compiled by author.

gas and home heating oil prices would be correlated strongly and as such, an estimate of cross elasticity for price of gas arrived at by excluding the price of home heating oil would include, partly at least, the effects of substitution between electricity and home heating oil also.

Halvorsen[9] found the difference in elasticities obtained from a static model using cross-sectional data and from a number of dynamic formulations to be negligible. This apparently was the result of cross-sectional data used having been representative of the differences over time. A static adjustment model would be suitable for simulation purposes if a steady trend were expected in prices and income. However, an assumption of steady trends not only would be invalidated by the trends of the mid-1970s but also would limit the scope of the model. Hence, for this purpose, a nine-year inverted geometric lag response has been assumed for the effects of prices as well as incomes in the residential sector. This lag structure was adopted because in Halvorsen's study it seemed to provide plausible estimates of elasticities. The form of the price-income lagged effect is shown in Figure 2.1. It increases geometrically up to the midpoint of the total lag period and then declines geometrically until the end of the nine years. Then for any time interval t the effect of prices at the start of t would be

$$P_t^L = \frac{\alpha}{2}\{[P_{t-1}(1-\alpha)^{T-1} + P_{t-2}(1-\alpha)^{T-2} + \cdots + P_{t-T}] + [P_{t-T-1} + P_{t-T-2}(1-\alpha) + P_{t-T-3}(1-\alpha)^2 + \cdots + P_{t-2T}(1-\alpha)^{T-1}]\}$$

where

$P_t^L \equiv$ the total effect of prices at the start of time interval t,

$\alpha \equiv$ a weighting constant characterizing the nature of the effect, and

$T \equiv$ total number of time intervals in the lag period.

The above expression for P_t^L can be written as

$$P_t^L = \frac{\alpha}{2}(P_t' + P_t'')$$

where

$$P_t' = P_{t-1}(1-\alpha)^{T-1} + P_{t-2}(1-\alpha)^{T-2} + \cdots + P_{t-T} \qquad (2.1)$$

and

$$P_t'' = P_{t-T-1} + P_{t-T-2}(1-\alpha) + \cdots + P_{t-2T}(1-\alpha)^{T-1}. \qquad (2.2)$$

Multiplying equation (2.1) by $(1-\alpha)$ we get

$$P_t'(1-\alpha) = P_{t-1}(1-\alpha)^T + P_{t-2}(1-\alpha)^{T-1} + P_{t-3}(1-\alpha)^{T-2}$$
$$+ \cdots + P_{t-T}(1-\alpha)$$

but $P_{t-1}' = P_{t-2}(1-\alpha)^{T-1} + P_{t-3}(1-\alpha)^{T-2} + \cdots + P_{t-T-1}$.

Subtracting P_{t-1}' from $P_t'(1-\alpha)$ gives

$$P_t'(1-\alpha) - P_{t-1}' = P_{t-1}(1-\alpha)^T - P_{t-T-1}$$

$$P_t' = \frac{(P_{t-1}' - P_{t-T-1})}{1-\alpha} + P_{t-1}(1-\alpha)^{T-1}. \qquad (2.3)$$

Thus, in any time period t, the value of P_t' can be determined if P_{t-1}', P_{t-T-1}, and P_{t-1} are known.

Similarly, from equation (2.2) we know

$$P_t'' = P_{t-T-1} + P_{t-T-2}(1-\alpha) + P_{t-T-3}(1-\alpha)^2 + \cdots + P_{t-2T}(1-\alpha)^{T-1}$$

and

$$P''_{t-1} = P_{t-T-2} + P_{t-T-3}(1-\alpha) + P_{t-T-4}(1-\alpha)^2 + \cdots$$
$$+ P_{t-2T-1}(1-\alpha)^{T-1}$$

Then multiplying P''_{t-1} by $(1-\alpha)$ and subtracting from P''_t gives

$$P''_t - P''_{t-1}(1-\alpha) = P_{t-T-1} - P_{t-2T-1}(1-\alpha)^T$$

$$P''_t = P''_{t-1}(1-\alpha) + P_{t-T-1} - P_{t-2T-1}(1-\alpha)^T \qquad (2.4)$$

The last term on the right-hand side of equation (2.4) can be ignored since it is small enough to start with and will get progressively smaller being multiplied by $(1-\alpha)$ from one time interval to the next. From equation (2.4) one can see that if the values of P''_{t-1}, P_{t-T-1} are known, one can calculate the value of P''_t at the start of any time interval t.

Hence, using the values obtained from equations (2.3) and (2.4), the total effect of prices can be determined at the start of any time interval $t-1$, t, $t+1$, and so on. The change in consumption of electricity as a result of change in long run price effect would be given by

$$\Delta Q = \eta_{pp} \cdot Q_{t-1} \cdot \frac{\Delta P}{P^L_{t-1}}$$

where

$$\Delta P = P^L_t - P^L_{t-1}$$

$$P^L_{t-1} = \frac{\alpha}{2}(P'_{t-1} + P''_{t-1})$$

$$P^L_t = \frac{\alpha}{2}(P'_t + P''_t)$$

Q_{t-1} ≡ electricity consumption in previous period (t - 1) and

η_{pp} ≡ long run price elasticity of demand for electricity.

By using the expressions developed above, the change in electricity demand can be computed from one time interval to the next in response to changes in price. In this study, the lag structure of response to all price and income changes in the residential sector and to price changes in the commercial sector has been assumed to be similar. Thus the effects of changes in the price of gas as well as per capita income are calculated in exactly the same manner as for price of electricity, the only difference being the substitution of initial values and elasticities relevant in each case. Then the kilowatt hour per customer in each rate group is calculated progressively as a function of the changes in prices of electricity and gas, respectively, and changes in per capita income and a time trend; the initial values of kilowatt hour per customer of course must be specified at the start of the simulation run. The total change in kilowatt hour per customer as a result of changes in all the determining factors is the sum of all the individual changes, when small changes only are considered. The total demand in the residential sector for any time interval is merely the sum of all the products of kilowatt hour per customer and number of customers in each rate group.

INDUSTRIAL SECTOR

The specification of the primary equation for demand for electricity in the industrial sector is based on the work of Fisher and Kaysen[10] and Wilson[11] described earlier. This equation is of the form

$$D = KX^\beta \cdot (C/P)^\alpha \cdot (F/P)^\gamma$$

where

$D \equiv$ the total demand for electricity in the industrial sector,
$X \equiv$ output of the industrial sector in terms of value added in constant dollars,
$C \equiv$ price of coal,
$P \equiv$ price of electricity available commercially to the industrial sector, and
$F \equiv$ price of fuel oil.

α, β, and γ are constant parameters representing elasticities in each case.

Both Halvorsen[12] and Wilson (in some of the formulations estimated by him) have used absolute prices instead of price ratios for coal and electricity and for fuel oil and electricity, respectively. However, Wilson's particular estimation using such price ratios appears plausible and has been adopted in the above specification. If $\beta = 1$ (as was found suitable in our model on the basis described later), then

$$D/X = K \cdot (C/P)^\alpha \cdot (F/P)^\gamma$$

where D/X would measure kilowatt hour/value added.

In such a relationship it would be reasonable to assume that in the long run an industry would base its decisions on demand for electricity not purely on the absolute price of electricity but on the ratios included in the above model, because the extent of substitution in favor of directly using coal or oil as well as for generating electricity internally (which would use coal and oil primarily) would depend on these price ratios. Further, the regression results obtained by Wilson using these price ratios give particularly high credence to this specification.

Then with the equation described above, change in the value of kilowatt hour/value added will be given by

$$\Delta(D/X) = [\alpha \cdot \Delta(C/P)/C/P + \gamma \cdot \Delta(F/P)/F/P] D/X$$

α and γ in this case are the elasticities of demand for electricity per dollar of value added with respect to relative prices of coal and electricity and fuel oil and electricity, respectively. Thus, for every time interval, the change in kilowatt hour/value added can be computed using the changes in relative prices C/P and F/P and the values of α and γ.

The total demand for electricity in this sector will be a product of value added and kilowatt hour/value added. Actually a much more accurate measure would have been obtained by (1) determining the output of each industry, (2) finding out the kilowatt hour demand per unit output for each industry, (3) computing the product of (1) and (2) for each industry, and (4) summing up all the products obtained in (3). However, lack of data did not permit development of this approach; hence demand in this sector was investigated only for the aggregate of all industries in the region.

The computation of value added is designed to provide a means for measuring industrial output, which actually is the aggregate of disparate units of different goods produced. Value added can be computed if one knows at least one of the inputs to the production function as well as the overall coefficient relating that input to the output. For a single input production function, the coefficient naturally must be a proxy for all the other inputs; hence, over time it would change. This change would be the result of changes in technology, change in the capital/labor ratio, and other inputs. Hence for each time interval this single-input coefficient must be known, or at least its rate of change over time must be specified as also its initial value for a particular time interval.

In this model, employment has been used as the single input and the rate of change of the coefficient A has been determined as a function of time. Then, value added is given by

$$VA = A(t) \cdot L$$

where $L \equiv$ employment in the industrial sector and $A(t) \equiv$ the production coefficient, which is a function of time. Total value added obtained as above is then multiplied by kilowatt hour/value added, thereby yielding the total demand for electricity in the industrial sector. The effect of locational choice in response to prices of electricity has been emphasized earlier. In dealing with the nation as a whole this effect would be irrelevant because if industries from one region were to move into another that offers electricity at a lower price, then one region's loss is another's gain, as Wilson pointed out.[13] However, for a specific region this effect could be extremely important, since the mix of industries could alter the figure significantly for kilowatt hour/value added. In this study it was not considered necessary to include the locational effect explicitly, since the elasticities estimated by Wilson (and used herein) already include the effects, if any, of change in industry mix in response to prices of electricity.

COMMERCIAL SECTOR

The commercial sector in the Carolina Power and Light system (and this largely applies to other utilities also) is really a misnomer. It consists of a large number of rate groups from small businesses to apartment housing with single metering and is really a sector consisting of all other types of customers except residential and industrial. However, total electricity demand in this sector is less than one-third the total; and some individual rate groups within it are insignificant in comparison with the total demand for the whole system. It was decided to aggregate the separate rate groups into larger subgroups, so each subgroup would represent, as far as possible, some homogeneous activity. The subgroups used in the model consist of

(1) businesses of all types in the region;
(2) schools, educational institutions, and recreational facilities;
(3) churches;
(4) single-metered apartment housing and rural farm groups; and
(5) housing construction.

The purpose of demarcating these separate groups was to enable prediction of the level of activity within each on an economic basis. This activity would be reflected directly in the number of customers, assuming no changes in size take place over a period of time different from those observed in recent years. There is reason to believe that considerable increase has taken place in the average size of schools and educational institutions in recent years. However, the regression results described in subsequent sections yield a plausible set of relationships to determine the number of customers in any group. A large number of formulations were tried in this respect, since activity in the above-mentioned groups would be expected to be determined by variables such as total personal income in the region, per capita income, total population, and increase in population in a particular time period over the previous time period.

The electricity demand per customer in this sector would be subject to more or less the same forces as act on a household in the residential sector. The one difference lies in the fact that households have to act under an income constraint, whereas a unit in the commercial sector would not have a similar income constraint. In fact, in the case of a business establishment, for instance, its own income through increased sales conceivably could be a function of increased consumption of electricity, such as for neon signs and display gadgetry. Hence a customer unit in this sector can be assumed to be affected in its electricity demand decisions by (1) price of electricity, (2) price of gas, and (3) a time trend as a proxy for other variables such as display styles, established standards in space heating and cooling, changes in working hours, and so on. Consequently changes in kilowatt hour per customer in each subgroup are computed as a result of changes in price of electricity, price of gas, and a time trend.

The product of kilowatt hour per customer and number of customers when summed over all the subgroups gives the total demand for electricity in the commercial sector.

STATISTICAL METHODS

The first problem encountered in the collection and use of data typically arose on account of the fact that the areas served by Carolina Power and Light do not follow state or county lines. The problem, therefore, called for a basis for using economic and demographic data (which are only published by counties and states in known publications) to apply precisely to the Carolina Power and Light region. Fortunately, state government sources had available some estimates of the percentage of the total population of every county served by the utility. Hence these estimates were used for scaling countywide data on a pro-rata basis. Undoubtedly in some counties such pro-rating would introduce serious biases; for instance, if only 10 percent of the population of a county was served by Carolina Power and Light and this included a very large industrial plant, straightforward pro-rating would yield a lower estimate of industrial activity for this part of the county, particularly if the county as a whole is not highly industrialized. However, this error is equally likely to fall on the higher side as on the lower side, and with a total of 47 counties served by Carolina Power and Light either wholly or partly it may not be unreasonable to assume that on the aggregate for the region these errors would cancel out. Further, since comparable data for South Carolina counties were not available, it has been assumed that there are no differences in economic activity between North and South Carolina counties included in the composite region. This again may not cause any serious error, because it was found that 77 percent of the Carolina Power and Light system lies in North Carolina, and that 24.68 percent of the total population of this state is served directly by Carolina Power and Light. It has been assumed in the study that these percentages will not change over time. In addition to direct sales to customers in the residential, industrial, and commercial sectors, Carolina Power and Light also sells electricity to municipalities and cooperatives, who in turn sell electric power to small areas within their operational control. It was not possible to obtain data pertaining to these second-stage customers to include them as a separate sector in the model. In fact, in most cases it was not even known to how many customers a particular cooperative was reselling electricity. However, since these areas represent populations and activities much within the overall geographic region served by Carolina Power and Light, there is reason to believe that given comparable prices of electricity, these pockets of resale would behave no differently from the entire Carolina Power and Light region. As such, the growth path of electricity demand for resale by public authorities can be expected to follow the same percentage changes as the path for total direct sales to customers in the three sectors mentioned above. The statistical steps taken in estimating the entire model are discussed in the following sections.

Residential Sector

To estimate the relationship for percentage of customers in the high consumption group during a particular time interval, the following independent variables were specified with the percentage of customers in the high consumption group as the dependent variable in each case:

(1) kilowatt hour per customer in the medium consumption group and a time trend;

(2) kilowatt hour per customer in the high consumption group, kilowatt hour per customer in the medium consumption group, and a time trend; and
(3) kilowatt hour per customer in the high consumption group and a time trend.

Time series data were available from the North Carolina Utilities Commission, from which percentages and kilowatt hour per customer were calculated for each customer group for the years 1965-72. A fourth rate group was in existence in the company's rate structure but was abolished in 1970. Hence for 1965-70, percentages were calculated after excluding the fourth group. The results of OLS regressions obtained are shown in Table 2.1.

The figures shown in parentheses in Table 2.1 are standard errors of estimates in each case. Similar regressions were run for the percentage of customers in the medium consumption group as dependent variable. The results of estimation by OLS for these equations are given in Table 2.2.

TABLE 2.1

Estimation of Customers in High Consumption Group

	Equation (2.1)	Equation (2.2)	Equation (2.3)
KwH/customer in high consumption group		-0.1404^d (0.11423)	-0.216534^c (0.075535)
KwH/customer in medium consumption group	-1.389171^c (0.54572)	-0.70184^d (0.77803)	
Constant	14.3393^b (4.062)	11.61848^c (4.546213)	7.6942696^b (1.29575)
Time trend— annual	2.020316^a (0.1848776)	1.88126^a (0.2146)	1.6958617^a (0.0606)
R^2	0.996539	0.997502	0.996994

[a] Significant at the 0.1 percent level.
[b] Significant at the 5 percent level.
[c] Significant at the 10 percent level.
[d] Not significant.

Source: Compiled by the author.

TABLE 2.2

Estimation of Customers in Medium Consumption Group

	Coefficients Estimated in		
	Equation (2.1)	Equation (2.2)	Equation (2.3)
KwH/customer in medium consumption group		-0.99194^d (0.61173566)	-1.280274^c (0.57021872)
KwH/customer in low consumption group	-2.2744^d (1.295984)	-1.405979 (1.2488)	
Constant	65.940198^a (3.721542)	70.83221^a (4.4638765)	68.940373^a (4.244745)
Time trend— annual	1.278556^b (0.375151)	1.35707^b (0.33183)	1.0497956^a (0.19372956)
R^2	0.972454	0.98316810	0.97783421

[a] Significant at the 1 percent level.
[b] Significant at the 5 percent level.
[c] Significant at the 15 percent level.
[d] Not significant.

Source: Compiled by author.

In the cases represented in Tables 2.1 and 2.2, the third equation was adopted in both cases, since not only was the explained variation satisfactory in each case but the level of significance of the estimated coefficients also was much better.

The percentage of customers in the low consumption group is merely the difference between 100 percent and the sum of percentages in the other groups. Hence the percentage in the low consumption group was not estimated directly but was derived only as a difference in the final model. All the estimates were, of course, converted to apply to a DT of two months.

The average size of household was determined on the basis of data for North Carolina published in the North Carolina Statistical Abstract 1973. These were available only for 1960 and 1970, and hence a straight line trend was estimated for changes in average household size. In his study of long run residential demand Halvorsen[14] included household size as an independent variable, and he obtained a negative relationship between household size and total demand in the residential sector. This would result from our simulation model as well, since a larger household size would reduce the total number of customers and therefore total demand in the residential sector as well.

In calculating the kilowatt hour per customer in each group, estimates are required of prices of electricity, gas, per capita income, and the time trend in each group. Electricity prices (revenue/total kilowatt hours) were available month by month for the three Carolina Power and Light residential rate groups for the period 1965-73. These were used after discounting with the consumer price index in the simulation runs, since only real prices in the model were used and certain assumptions were made regarding their increase during the period beyond 1973-90. Gas prices were available for the years 1965, 1970, and 1971 in the North Carolina Statistical Abstract 1973[*] and for 1974 from the North Carolina Utilities Commission. Weighted averages of these prices were used to allow for differences in price and extent of sales for different companies for the intervening periods between the years mentioned above; a straight line variation was assumed and prices estimated for each two-month period. Per capita income was again available from the North Carolina Statistical Abstract 1973 for a number of years through 1972. All the values used in the model were, of course, converted to real values by dividing by the consumer price index, with 1967 as the base year. Thus, all the values used for prices and incomes in the model are in terms of 1967 dollars.

Halvorsen estimated a time trend of negative 1 percent a year in his long run model described above. This value was used in the model, and the values obtained by simulation were compared with actual observations for the validation period mid-1968 to end-1973. The inclusion of Halvorsen's value in this model worked well for the high consumption group, giving an error in kilowatt hours per customer well under 1 percent for the terminal period in 1973. However, for the medium and low consumption groups the errors were of the order of 6-8 percent. One reason for this phenomenon could be that the national data used for estimation of the Halvorsen model is closer to the characteristics of the high consumption group in the Carolina Power and Light region than the lower two groups. Hence it was decided to use time trend variables for these two groups whose values were based on the simulation run, but Halvorsen's estimate was

---

[*] The North Carolina State Government Statistical Abstract is prepared and periodically updated by the Statistical Services Section, Office of State Budget, Department of Administration, North Carolina State Government, Raleigh, North Carolina.

retained for the high consumption group. The values obtained in the medium and low consumption groups were 0.14 percent and 0.23 percent for each DT. These were selected after considerable trial and error, so values of kilowatt hours per customer produced by simulation yielded the minimum squared sum of deviations for selected points in the 1968-73 period.

The values of elasticity of demand with respect to electricity price, gas price, and income, respectively, were those estimated by Halvorsen in his model referred to above. The biases likely in these estimates have been discussed earlier, but they seemed by far the most reliable existing in the literature today. The biggest doubt stemming from the use of these elasticity estimates is whether they can be assumed to remain constant over a wide range of conditions and price and income changes. Halvorsen's estimates, as all others available, are based on data pertaining to a period when electricity prices were declining steadily. Whether elasticities incorporating long run changes from that observed period will continue to hold even when prices increase is a matter for further research using suitable data. In this book, however, the implication has been built in that the market for used appliances and electricity-using devices is as perfect as that for new ones. Thus consumers will respond similarly to price changes, whatever the directions of such changes may be.

The most difficult estimation in the residential sector was in regard to population changes, particularly migration. For determining changes in death rates a straight line trend was assumed, since it was felt that a relationship based on economic variables would be difficult to specify. Again, data from the North Carolina Statistical Abstract 1973 were used for estimating this trend. The data available were in respect of resident deaths for 1950, 1960, 1965, 1970, and 1972. These were converted to death rates per 1,000 using total population data from the same abstract. The trend thus established, showing a change in death rate by 0.0000111 per thousand for every DT, has been used in the simulations.

The relationship determining birth rates for the region was estimated using different alternative forms by OLS as follows. Resident live births for North Carolina are published in the North Carolina Statistical Abstracts (1971 and 1973 editions). These absolute figures were taken and converted to birth rates per 1,000 population for the years 1940, 1950, 1960, 1965, 1969, 1970, and 1972. Birth rate per 1,000 was specified as the dependent variable in all the formulations. The independent variables in each alternative equation were (1) real per capita income, (2) real per capital income and a time trend, and (3) real per capita income and percentage of urban population to the total. Data for these variables were available in the abstracts mentioned above for the relevant years. Values of per capita income

TABLE 2.3

Estimation of Birth Rate

	Estimates Obtained with		
	Equation (2.1)	Equation (2.2)	Equation (2.3)
Real per capita income	-0.00000294^b (0.00000109)	-0.000122899^c (0.0006898)	-0.000247^c (0.0006623)
Time trend		-0.00012474^c (0.00049628)	
Percentage of urban to total population			-0.00005947^c (0.000831)
Constant	0.02709020^a (0.00239329)	0.02619^a (0.004559)	0.02850287^c (0.0199156)
R^2	0.59255481	0.59889036	0.59307595

[a]Significant at the one-tenth of 1 percent level.
[b]Significant at the 10 percent level.
[c]Not significant.

Source: Compiled by author.

were divided by the consumer price index to arrive at real values with 1967 as the base. Results of the OLS regressions are tabulated in Table 2.3. It should be observed that equation (2.1) yielded the most satisfactory values, although the value of R^2 was only 0.59255481.

Estimates for equation (2.1) have been adopted in the final model after dividing the coefficients to apply to a two-month interval DT. A search of the literature did not provide a better set of relationships that could be used in this study.

The problem with arriving at a relationship for migration lay in the paucity of time series data on population movements in to and out of the region. Therefore, only one equation was specified with migration as the dependent variable and two independent variables—namely (1) the lagged difference in real per capita income between the United States and North Carolina and (2) a lagged variable representing fractional growth in industrial employment over the previous year, which was used as a proxy variable representing growth in all types of employment. The only data that could be obtained were for migration pertaining to North Carolina and its counties for the periods 1950-60, 1960-65, and 1965-69, as published in Profile of North

Carolina Counties by the state government. These figures were converted on a pro-rata basis to apply to the scale of the Carolina Power and Light region. However, this sample of three sets of figures was not adequate; hence, two different cross sections were formed encompassing two sets of 10 counties in each case by pooling migration figures for the period 1965-69. This again was pro-rated by a scale factor in each case, which was the ratio of the total population of the Carolina Power and Light system to the population of the 10-county sample.

The lagged values of difference between the United States and North Carolina real per capita incomes were computed from data available in the North Carolina Statistical Abstract 1973. These were, of course, suitably divided by the consumer price index for each year, and a lag of two years introduced in relating them to the dependent variable—migration. The growth in industrial employment lagged by two years was calculated from data published by the Employment Security Commission of North Carolina in August 1971 as well as from the North Carolina Statistical Abstract 1973. These values were expressed as fractions of the base year employment level. OLS regression results for the migration equation are given in Table 2.4. Levels of significance were 20 percent for the constant term, 3 percent for the income differential coefficient, and 13 percent for the growth in employment coefficient.

It would be pertinent to mention that the value of migration for 1950-60 was a substantially large negative figure, since historically the Carolinas were a region for net out-migration and only recently has the trend reversed. As such the migration equation estimated above, in spite of not having a highly significant constant intercept, is capable of predicting net in- or out-migration for the region. Nevertheless, migration represents an activity that has considerable

TABLE 2.4

Estimation of Migration
$R^2 = 0.972226$

Constant Term	Estimated Coefficients for Difference in U.S. and N.C. per Capita Income	Fractional Growth in Industrial Employment
291954	-130.21714	1316773.18
(102371)	(16.2418)	(343644.65)

Source: Compiled by author.

scope for detailed investigation, since its effects would be spread over the entire economy of the region. For instance, to the extent that skills of different types are injected into the region by migration, there is accumulation of human capital taking place. This would have an effect on the growth characteristics of the region's future activity, and the measurement of this phenomenon would add considerably to the strength of any prediction.

INDUSTRIAL SECTOR

Industry in the region has been divided into seven major groups: namely, food and kindred products, textile mill products, apparel and other textile products, furniture and lumber, chemicals, machinery, and all others. No serious problems were encountered in estimation in the industrial sector within the framework of the equations specified.

First, for all seven industry groups, total employment levels and value added were extracted for North and South Carolina from the Survey of Current Business.* Four sets of values were computed for 1963, 1967, 1970, and 1971, correcting value added in terms of 1967 real dollars. The ratio of value added/(total employment) for each industry group was in effect the single-input coefficient discussed earlier. Using the observations for the four years stated above, the rate of change in this coefficient for each DT was estimated, assuming a straight line trend in each industry group. The initial value of total employment for mid-1968 was obtained from North Carolina Work Force Estimates 1971, published by the North Carolina Employment Security Commission. Again the value for North Carolina was prorated to apply to the Carolina Power and Light region.

Value added time series were obtained from the North Carolina Statistical Abstract 1973, and the initial value for the region was estimated for mid-1968 by pro-rating. Using this figure, kilowatt hour/value added was calculated for the region for mid-1968, the numerator being obtained from Carolina Power and Light data. Elasticities of demand that affect kilowatt hour/value added for one time interval to the next are those estimated by Wilson[15] in respect to price ratios for coal and electricity and fuel oil and electricity, respectively. Wilson's estimates, being based on cross-sectional data, are likely to be biased upward, since they would include

---

*Survey of Current Business is a publication of the U.S. Department of Commerce.

FORECASTING METHODOLOGY 45

locational effects as well. In that sense the estimates obtained in the simulation runs for employment levels in each industry group cannot be relied on totally. If the locational effect is substantial, considerable changes in industry mix can take place in response to changes in price. The result may be that although value added by manufacturing may not change significantly, employment by different industry groups probably would. Employment in this model is used only as a means to obtain value added.

Initial values for average electricity price to the industrial sector were obtained from North Carolina Utilities Commission past data, and prices for coal and fuel oil used in power generation (since self-generation of power is the substitute for commercially available electricity) were obtained from the Edison Electric Institute's Statistical Abstract for 1973. As price ratios are involved in this case, the values were used directly without division by the consumer price index.

COMMERCIAL SECTOR

Since a large number of rate groups are included in this sector, they were first aggregated to form five subgroups as follows:

(1) business group, consisting of four different rate groups;
(2) school and institution group, consisting of four different rate groups;
(3) church group, consisting of two different rate groups;
(4) commercial housing group, consisting of three different rate groups; and
(5) housing construction, which is a rate group by itself.

Average prices of electricity for each rate group were available for the years 1964-72, but weighted averages had to be computed to get values applicable to the aggregated subgroups. Prices for gas used in this sector were similar to those in the residential sector. Again real prices were used as inputs to the model.

The first step in estimation was to arrive at a set of relationships that would determine the number of customers in each subgroup. A number of equations were specified and estimated. Data used for the independent variables were in respect to total population, real total personal income, and real per capita income, all of which were available from the North Carolina Statistical Abstract 1973. Time series for the number of customers in each group for the period 1964-72 were constructed using North Carolina Utilities Commission data.

Results obtained from OLS for the above subgroup customers are shown in Tables 2.5 through 2.9.

TABLE 2.5

Estimation of Business Subgroup Customers

	Coefficients Estimated for Equation (2.1)	Equation (2.2)
Total population	0.06161455[b] (0.02933532)	—
Total personal income	—	0.932255704[a] (0.55281988)
Per capita income	2.52535168[b] (9.56038842)	—
Constant	-39351.53774[b] (20620.5333)	24266.40575[a] (2320.32737)
R^2	0.98463532	0.98272183

[a] Significant at the 0.02 of 1 percent level.
[b] Not significant.

Source: Compiled by author.

TABLE 2.6

Estimation of School Subgroup Customers

	Coefficients Estimated in Equation (2.1)	Equation (2.2)	Equation (2.3)	Equation (2.4)
Total population	—	—	0.001038[c] (0.00494)	—
Total personal income	0.37941912[b] (0.068224)	0.397198[a] (0.05418)	0.00000026[c] (0.00000067)	0.168653 (0.581)
Time trend	—	—	—	52.2022[c] (132.01)
Increase in population over previous period	1.10951295[c] (2.1624)	—	—	—
Constant	286.8263[c] (260.5012)	243.5159[c] (227.4049)	-788.886[c] (4920.7)	1040.532[c] (2030.92)
R^2	0.92	0.9149	0.9158	0.918

[a] Significant at 0.2 of 1 percent level.
[b] Significant at the 1 percent level.
[c] Not significant.

Source: Compiled by author.

TABLE 2.7

Estimation of Church Subgroup Customers

	Coefficients Estimated in Equation (2.1)	Coefficients Estimated in Equation (2.2)
Total personal income	0.34975[a] (0.010356)	0.00000039[b] (0.00000007)
Constant	4011.1165[a] (42.3145)	4332.72597[b] (611.2903)
Total population	—	-0.0003067[c] (0.0005813)
R^2	0.99477	0.995

[a] Significant at the 0.02 of 1 percent level.
[b] Significant at the 1 percent level.
[c] Not significant.

Source: Compiled by author.

TABLE 2.8

Estimation of Housing Subgroup Customers

	Per Capita Income	Constant	R^2
Coefficients estimated for	6.022833[a] (1.2408)	-12472.4288[b] (3388.9335)	0.8548712

[a] Significant at the 2 percent level.
[b] Significant at the 5 percent level.

Source: Compiled by author.

TABLE 2.9

Estimation of Construction Subgroup Customers

	Coefficients Estimated in			
	Equation (2.1)	Equation (2.2)	Equation (2.3)	Equation (2.4)
Per capita income	3.520735[b] (1.09879)	−0.191403[c] (2.31684)	4.25159[b] (1.3164)	4.38316[a] (1.0489)
Total population	—	0.011817[c] (0.008366)	—	—
Increase in population over previous period	−0.45955[c] (14.389)	—	—	—
Increase in population over previous period—lagged	—	—	3.49089[c] (14.39)	—
Constant	−5454.254[c] (2776.53)	−13900.357[c] (7194.107)	−7612.389[c] (3459.03)	−7881.649[b] (2864.895)
R^2	0.7682	0.8493	0.817	0.8136

[a] Significant at the 5 percent level.
[b] Significant at the 10 percent level.
[c] Not significant.

Source: Compiled by author.

From the results tabulated above, estimated equations were adopted for the model as follows:

(a) equation (2.2) for the business subgroup,
(b) equation (2.2) for the school and educational institute subgroup,
(c) equation (2.1) for the church subgroup,
(d) the single equation estimated for commercial housing subgroup, and
(e) equation (2.4) for the housing construction subgroup.

The estimates were, of course, multiplied suitably to make them applicable to two-month values.

FORECASTING METHODOLOGY

The computation of kilowatt hours per customer for each subgroup is a function of electricity and gas prices as described earlier. Estimates for elasticities used are those obtained by Halvorsen.[16] The time trend variable, however, has been adopted after a set of simulation trials to ensure that the values adopted minimize the squared deviations for the period 1968-72. Final time trend values incorporated in the model are

(a) business subgroup—0.6 percent per DT,
(b) school subgroup—1.6 percent per DT,
(c) church subgroup—1.18 percent per DT,
(d) housing subgroup—3.72 percent per DT,
(e) housing construction subgroup—3.43 percent per DT.

It must be mentioned in concluding this section that although the model used in this equation is really a simultaneous equation system, none of the relationships estimated is affected by the econometric problems involved in simultaneity. This happens because variables such as total personal income have been assumed to be exogenous. This may not be totally implausible because the feedback effect of the variables determining electricity demand on total income of the region would be very small indeed.

DESCRIPTION OF THE DYNAMIC SIMULATION MODEL

The first part of the program consists of dimension and equivalence statements and other statements defining values of certain variables required for the subroutines used in the program. The section titled "Model Data" consists of prices of gas and electricity; price ratios for coal and electricity and fuel oil and electricity, respectively; per capita income and growth rates assumed for the simulation period. These values are in respect to actual data for the period mid-1968 to end-1973 except for growth rates, which come into effect only after 1973 in the simulation runs. Data that were available directly for each two-month period from January 1964 to December 1973, such as residential sector prices, have been fed in by calling the ARRAY subroutine, but others for which annual data only were available have been read in by a series of DO-LOOPS after estimating changes within a year on a linear basis. The necessity for feeding in data for at least four and one-half years before the initial period of mid-1968 arose because of the nine-year lagged effect of prices and incomes. Subroutine ECOEFF, which was developed to compute these effects, utilizes prices for each time interval within the latter half of the total lag period, along with the initial value of the relevant weighted average.

A set of exogenous values has been adopted to drive the model. The growth rates of total personal income, GROWTH, for this region and U.S. per capita income, PCINGR, have been based on a forecast for the United States and its constituent regions, published in the Survey of Current Business.[17] For the sensitivity analysis, described later, these values have been varied to assess the effects of such variations on both demand and supply. The rates of growth of real prices of electricity and its substitutes also have been treated as exogenous variables. Forecasts for long range changes in coal and fuel oil prices were furnished by an unpublished study on the subject by a major consulting firm.[18] The price of natural gas has been assumed to grow at the same rate as that of fuel oil. The forecast referred to above indicated growth of prices in terms of a low range, a high range, and the most probable growth path. For the base prediction runs with our model, the high range values were adopted, which amount to an exponential uniform growth rate of 0.9 percent, respectively, for coal and fuel oil for every DT. It was not possible to obtain any forecasts for growth of electricity prices, since not only have these grown unpredictably in the recent past but also these have been included in the model first by using a set of future estimates, which this author regards as most "reasonable," and then by varying them to study the effects of different electricity prices on the entire system. It must also be mentioned that the values adopted for coal and fuel oil cannot be accepted as sacrosanct, particularly in view of the current "energy crisis" and its uncertain long run effects.

Following this section of the model, initial values have been specified for the three sectors. Since the model was initialized for the time interval July-August 1968, all the initial values entered pertain to that particular time interval. However, should the need arise and given the appropriate values, the model can be run with a different starting period.

At the end of the section for initial values, the PREPC subroutines have been called for the simulation runs. The function performed by and the details involved in these standard FORDYN subroutines have not been discussed herein, because a thorough and detailed discussion has been presented in R. W. Llewellyn's book FORDYN,[19] from which all except the ECOEFF subroutine have been used. The section titled "Time Related Data" merely picks up the appropriate prices for each iteration period from the array of data fed in exogenously as described earlier.

DOMESTIC SECTOR

A flow chart showing the interrelationships between some of the main variables in this sector is presented as Figure 2.2. The only average calculated in this sector, PCIDIA, is the smoothed average of the difference between U.S. per capita income and the region's per capita income. This was provided because in the migration equation PCIDIA is an important variable, for which it is reasonable to assume that a single-period value alone would not enter the decision-making function; a decision to migrate normally would be based on a smoothed average of income comparisons between the region and the rest of the nation.

The levels calculated in this sector are the total population TOPO1L, which is added to or subtracted from by the flows of births, deaths, and migration. The number of households or residential customers TOHO1L is a level determined by TOPO1L and the average household size HHSZ1V. The levels of customers in each rate group are determined next by multiplication of TOHO1L by the variables CHRGIV, CMRGIV, and CLRGIV, respectively, which represent the fraction of customers in each rate group during a particular time interval.

Auxiliary variables calculated are average household size HHSZ1V, which changes in each time interval by the trend HHTR1V, which was estimated and entered in the initial value equations. Next, a series of calls of the subroutine titled ECOEFF is made to calculate the effect of real electricity prices in each rate group, the effects of real per capita income, and the effects of gas prices on each rate group. Since subroutine ECOEFF has been devised in this study specifically to deal with the nine-year inverted-V lagged effect of prices and incomes, a brief explanation of how it works would be relevant. The inputs required to be specified for each time period while calling the subroutine are

(1) the weighted sum of the influencing variable (that is, price or income) for the declining part of the inverted-V acting on a particular time interval;

(2) the weighted sum of the same influencing variable for the increasing part of the inverted-V;

(3) the last (most recent) single period value of the influencing variable;

(4) the inverse of the weighting constant used for the lagged effect;

FIGURE 2.2

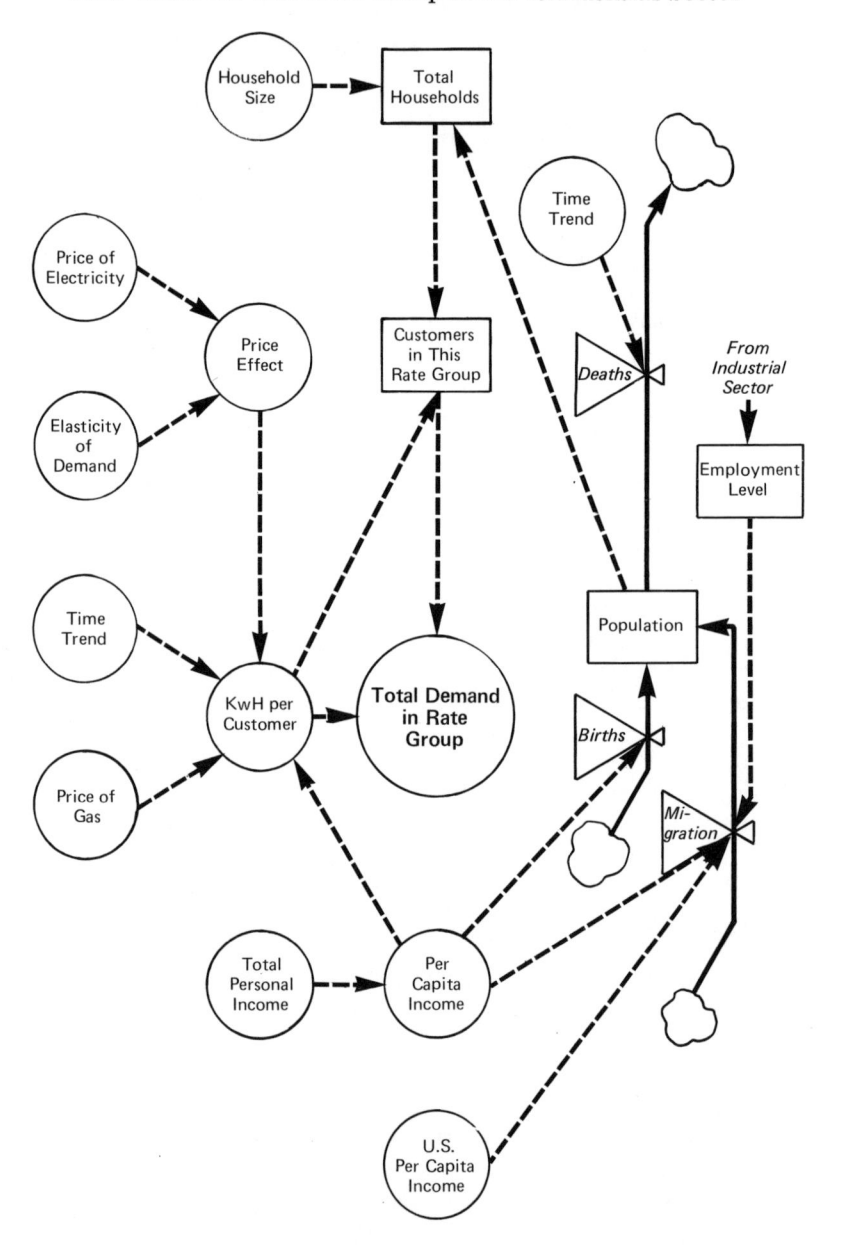

Flow Chart for One Rate Group in the Residential Sector

Source: Compiled by author.

FORECASTING METHODOLOGY

(5) the long run elasticity of demand pertinent to a particular call of the subroutine;

(6) the array of prices or incomes for each interval in the latter part of the inverted-V lag period; and

(7) the total length of the lag.

The subroutine has a built-in Boxcar arrangement by which in every call it throws out the value of the influencing variable, which no longer has any effect, and takes in the most recent value of the variable to calculate a change in the total equivalent effect for the particular time interval. The calculation carried out is exactly the same as described earlier in relation to the mathematics of the lagged effect of prices and incomes.

Once the calls of subroutine ECOEFF have calculated the change in demand for electricity (in percentage terms) over the values of the previous time interval, the aggregate effect due to prices of electricity and gas and per capita income is computed in the next series of equations. These give values of ELDH1V, ELDM1V, and ELDL1V, which represent kilowatt hours per customer in each rate group for the particular time interval. DOEL1V is then the total kilowatt hours demand for the residential sector for the particular DT interval. The next auxiliary variables calculated are the fractions of customers in each rate group, the relationships for which were estimated and described earlier. A set of IF statements allows total personal income to be calculated separately as (1) exogenously given values up to the middle of 1972 using real data and (2) a function of the exogenously assumed growth rate beyond this period, up to 1990.* Per capita income, PCIN1V, for the region for each DT is merely the quotient of TOPINC, total personal income divided by TOPO1L, the total population of the region. Per capita income for the United States, PCINNV, is calculated as a function of the exogenous growth rate assumed earlier.

The rates calculated in this sector of the model are in respect to flows of people, that is, the rates of births, deaths, and migration for each DT. Birth rate is determined by the relationship estimated and described earlier and death rate by the linear trend estimated for this purpose. However, the calculation of migration consists of two parts—first the migration decision rate is based on the equation estimated earlier, then the rate thus calculated passes through a third-order exponential delay of two years in duration, and the outflow from this delay represents actual migration during the particular time interval. This delay in the flow of migration is in keeping with the

---

*The IF function is used commonly in Fortran computer language.

estimation procedure followed for the purpose, wherein a two-year lag had been assumed in the specified relationship. In essence, the introduction of a delay achieves the same effect.

INDUSTRIAL SECTOR

Two smoothed averages are calculated in this sector in respect to the price ratios of coal to electricity and fuel oil to electricity. Although the values of elasticities used to calculate the effects of changes in these price ratios were estimated by Wilson on the basis of cross-sectional data, smoothed values have been used in the model to render the relationship more plausible. In effect the application of smoothed values implies a weighted average of price ratios affecting demand for electricity.

Levels of employment in each industry group are calculated, based on the rate of growth assumed. These growth rates are based on the forecasts made in the study published in the Survey of Current Business.[20] The forecast was used to obtain a linear growth in employment for each industry group, so terminal values for 1990 are in keeping with the published study. The total employment in this sector is merely the sum of the levels in each industry group. Again, values used in this model for the period up to mid-1972 are based on actual employment statistics for the period, and the growth assumption comes into effect only subsequently, by means of a set of IF statements.

Auxiliary variables in this sector are calculated next. These include the smoothed change in price ratios and the related change in electricity demand EIRC2V and EIRF2V, using long run elasticities as multipliers. The single input coefficient for each of the seven groups is calculated next, based on the change in these coefficients estimated earlier. The kilowatt hours demanded per $1,000 of value added, ELVA2V, are calculated as a function of EIRC2V and EIRF2V and the value of ELVA2V in the previous period.

The rates equations included in this sector determine output in terms of value added in constant dollars by manufacturing. These are a function of the existing employment in each group and the single input coefficient thereof. The sum of value added in all seven groups is the value added by the entire sector.

A feature of the industrial sector in this model, which requires comment, is the fact that there is no endogenous feedback from any other sector into this one, although the fractional increase in employment GREM2V in this sector is one of the determinants of migration in the residential sector. The feedback or link between the two sectors

FIGURE 2.3

Flow Chart for One Industry Group in the Industrial Sector

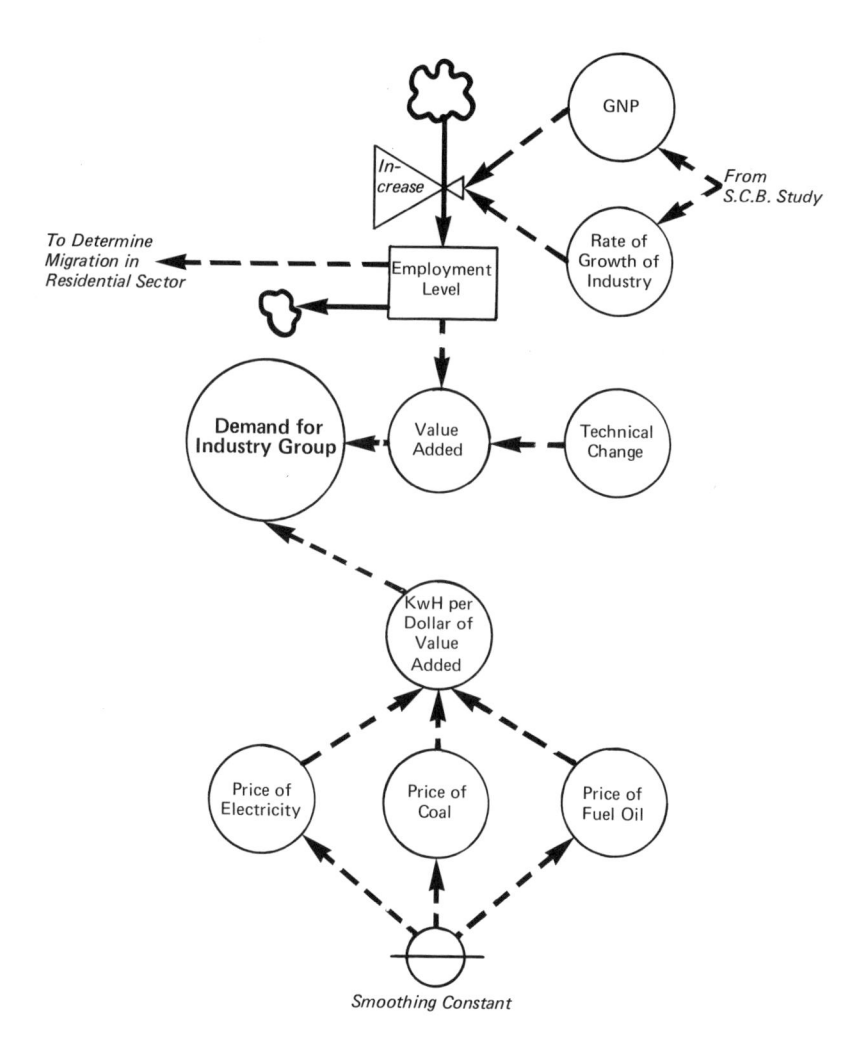

Source: Compiled by author.

nevertheless exists further in an overt manner, since the growth rates for total personal income and industrial employment come from the same composite study, which uses the two variables in an interdependent way. Some attempts were made to find a relationship between the total value added by industry and total personal income in the region, but nothing significant was revealed. Such a relationship might require an elaborate formulation of a growth model and its estimation, which is beyond the scope of the present study. A simple flow diagram for the industrial sector is shown as Figure 2.3.

COMMERCIAL SECTOR

The level equations in the commercial sector determine the number of customers in each of the five subgroups. These equations were described in the previous section, and a change in the levels from one time interval to the next is a function of total personal income in three cases and per capita income in the other two.

The auxiliary variables are calculated next and include a set of five calls of subroutine ECOEFF, each call computing the effect of prices of electricity on electricity demand within the particular group. The kilowatt hours per customer in each group—ELBU3V, ELSC3V, ELCH3V, ELHO3V, and ELCO3V, respectively—is calculated as a function of this price effect, the effect of gas prices, and a time trend. The effect of gas prices ELGP1V was calculated in the residential sector and is applied to each subgroup in the commercial sector as well. The time trend in each case was estimated as a result of simulation runs as described in the previous section.

There are no rates to be calculated in this sector. The total demand for electricity is given herein by TOCO3V, which is the sum of demand in all five subgroups. A flow chart for the commercial sector is shown in Figure 2.4. The relationships described above and as indicated in the flow chart are essentially simple. Again, there is no feedback in the model on how activity in the commercial sector affects demographic-economic variables in the other sectors. This is one of the areas in which there is considerable room for further research, but that would require the estimation of a complete growth model for the region.

FIGURE 2.4

Flow Chart for the Commercial Sector

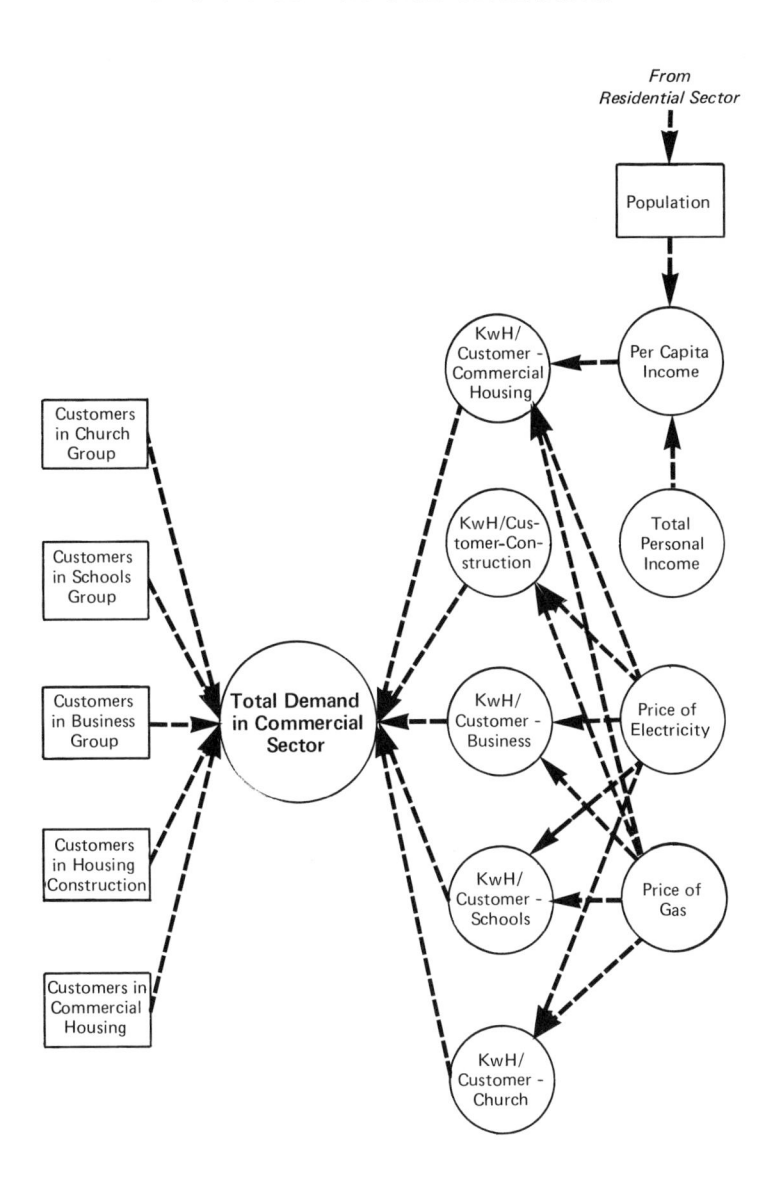

Source: Compiled by author.

NOTES

1. Jay W. Forrester, Industrial Dynamics (Cambridge, Mass.: Massachusetts Institute of Technology Press, 1961).
2. Ibid., p. 54.
3. Paul A. Samuelson, "Interactions Between the Multiplier Analysis and the Principle of Acceleration," in Readings in Macroeconomics, M. G. Mueller, ed. (New York: Holt, Rinehart and Winston, Inc., 1966).
4. Robert W. Llewellyn, FORDYN, An Industrial Dynamics Simulator (Raleigh, N.C.: private publication, 1965).
5. Jay W. Forrester, Urban Dynamics (Cambridge, Mass.: Massachusetts Institute of Technology Press, 1969).
6. Jay W. Forrester, World Dynamics (Cambridge, Mass.: Wright-Allen Press, 1971).
7. William D. Nordhaus, "World Dynamics: Measurement without Data," The Economic Journal, Vol. 83 (December 1973): 1156-83.
8. Robert Halvorsen, Long-Run Residential Demand for Electricity (Cambridge, Mass.: Environmental Systems Program, 1972).
9. Ibid.
10. Franklin M. Fisher and Carl Kaysen, A Study in Econometrics, The Demand for Electricity in the United States (Amsterdam, Holland: North Holland Publishing Company, 1962).
11. John W. Wilson, Residential and Industrial Demand for Electricity: An Empirical Analysis (Ann Arbor, Mich.: University Microfilms, Inc., 1969).
12. Robert Halvorsen, Demand for Electric Power in the United States, Discussion Paper 13-13 (Seattle: Institute for Economic Research, 1973).
13. Wilson, op. cit.
14. Halvorsen, Long-Run Demand, op. cit.
15. Wilson, op. cit.
16. Halvorsen, Demand for Electric Power, op. cit.
17. Henry L. Degraff, Robert D. Graham, Jr., and Edward A. Trott, Jr., "State Projections of Income, Employment, and Population," Survey of Current Business (April 1972).
18. Data taken from a classified study.
19. Llewellyn, op. cit.
20. Degraff et al., op. cit.

CHAPTER 3

SIMULATION RESULTS

The model was run to cover the period mid-1968 to end-1990 with a large variety of assumptions. The results of these runs are presented in this chapter with a view not only to tracing out the expected time path of important variables but also attempting to reveal the nature of the system that determines the values of these variables. The results are discussed, therefore, in two parts—the first consisting of the most likely forecast for the simulation time span and the second being an analysis of the sensitivity of the system as a function of changes in the exogenous variables.

FORECAST UP TO 1990

Economic-Demographic Variables

The real growth rate assumed in this run is as projected in the Survey of Current Business (SCB) study mentioned in Chapter 2. However, the percentage of total personal income for North Carolina in 1990 over that in 1969 is 243.45 percent, according to figures published in the study. Corresponding values obtained by simulation yield a percentage of 245.34 percent based on figures for mid-1969 and mid-1990, respectively. The difference arises because real data have been used in the model for the period 1968-72, and observed total personal income for 1972 was higher than would have been obtained with the growth rate envisaged in the SCB study.

Population in the SCB study for 1990 is 127.32 percent of the 1969 value. However, population predictions (which are determined endogenously in our model) yield a corresponding figure of 120.53 percent for mid-1990 values as a percentage of the mid-1969 values. Thus, population growth obtained in this study is significantly lower than the SCB study. Drops in birth rates observed in the last three years both in the United States as a whole and in North Carolina would tend to support a prediction lower than the SCB forecast for population in 1990.

Per capita income for the United States as a whole has been assumed to grow in this model at the same rate as the SCB forecast. This yields a 1990 value 181.8 percent of the 1969 value. However, per capita income for the Carolina Power and Light region grows more rapidly in the simulated results, being in 1990 a value 202.22 percent of the 1969 value, as against the corresponding SCB figure of 191.26 percent. The present study yields a per capita income prediction for the region of $910.00 per DT, which is equivalent to an annual rate of $5460.00. Correspondingly, the difference in per capita income between the United States and this region, which in mid-1968 was $684.00 per year, reduces to $624.00 per year by mid-1990. All incomes in this as well as the SCB study are measured in terms of 1967 dollars.

The migration equation used in this study is highly sensitive to the difference in per capita income between the United States and this region. This fact is revealed by the tests using different growth assumptions, described later. However, with the SCB assumption of regional growth, the pattern of migration remains fairly consistent over the period of the simulation run. The model starts with a period of in-migration at a rate of 2,200 per DT (time interval), or 13,200 a year. This increases slightly within the next year but then declines to an annual rate of only 126 by mid-1972. For the next 14 months the region experiences out-migration, which reaches a two-month rate of 553 in spring of 1973. However, this is reversed at the end of 1973, and there is again a period of in-migration, which reaches a rate of 4,092 a year in spring of 1975. Another period of gradual decline follows till in-migration falls to 191 per DT, or an equivalent annual rate of 1,146 by the end of 1983. There follows again a period of gradual increase culminating in an in-migration rate of 746 per DT, or 4,476 a year at the end of the simulation run in end-1990. Hence, it may be concluded on the basis of this forecast that the Carolina Power and Light region will continue to experience in-migration predominantly, which would contribute to overall growth of population in spite of declining birth rates.

Demand in the Residential Sector

The basis for the price increase assumptions affecting this sector have been mentioned earlier. The most probable rates of growth of real prices of coal and gas have been assumed on the basis of the unpublished study mentioned in Chapter 2—these are, respectively, 0.9 percent for both fuels per DT, in real terms, or an equivalent 5.52 percent a year. Electricity prices are assumed to grow at the same rate as coal prices. This is based on the assumption that price increases in coal will set the standards for price increases in other areas, such as labor and transmission costs. Of course the increasing use of nuclear generation is likely to lower the cost per kilowatt hour, but this may be offset to a large extent by the rapidly increasing costs of fuel oil, construction materials, and stricter environmental standards, which probably will become more stringent with the proliferation of nuclear power generation. In 1973, approximately 67 percent of Carolina Power and Light's power generation came from coal, 15 percent from nuclear, 12.5 percent from oil, and 3.5 percent from hydroelectric power. Based on present indications, coal will continue to be important in determining generation costs for at least another decade. With the uncertainty in future prices of electricity, there appeared no better assumption available than to peg these prices to the same projected rate of increase as that of coal prices. In fact, the average price of electricity in the last six months of 1974 has gone up much faster than the assumed 5.52 percent a year; but if one were to observe only long run trends, the average for the past ten years is much lower. At any rate, the price variables in our sensitivity runs have been varied to get a range of forecasts for demand. There is every reason to assume that the recently observed spurt in prices cannot be sustained over an extended period, and it is hoped that the overall long run trend will be in keeping with the assumptions in this simulation run.

The above discussion on the assumptions underlying the future prices of electricity used in the model has been presented only to emphasize the fact that the forecasts of demand related to them are as weak or as robust as the assumptions themselves. The financial factors on which electricity pricing decisions are based are evaluated and discussed in Part II, and an explicit treatment of them at this stage is being withheld for this reason.

The unique effect of lags in response to price and income changes can be seen in the values for kilowatt hours per customer in the three residential sector rate groups. In the high consumption group, this variable, ELDH1V, increases gradually from 3.26 thousand kilowatt hours until it reaches a peak value of 4.62 thousand kilowatt hours per DT in end-1973. Beyond this point, however, there is a steady decline to a level of 1.81 thousand kilowatt hours by end-1990. Thus, the value of ELDH1V in end-1990 is only 55.5 percent of its initial value. In the medium consumption rate group, correspondingly, ELDM1V increases gradually from 1.40 thousand kilowatt hours to a value of 1.76 per DT in mid-1974 but then declines to a terminal value of 1.15 in end-1990. This represents kilowatt hours per customer in 1990 for this group at a figure 82.14 percent of its initial value. In the low consumption group, ELDL1V goes up from 0.612 thousand kilowatt hours per customer to 0.858 in mid-1974 but then continues a gradual decline to 0.614 at the end of 1990, which is 100.33 percent of its initial value. Thus the low consumption rate group is the only one in which the terminal value is higher than the initial period kilowatt hours per customer.

The total demand for electricity in the residential sector, nevertheless, does show an increase at the end of the simulation period. Demand increases at a rapid rate up to mid-1973, but then there is a reduction in the rate of increase. The increase, however, does continue to a peak value of 983,000 thousand kilowatt hours per DT at end-1974. There is then a period of actual decline in demand, which lasts for about 18 months, to a value of 958,000. A slight increase follows for four months, followed by another four months of decline to a value of 954,000. From early 1977 onward, however, there is again an increase in demand that steadily continues to a value of 1,160,000 thousand kilowatt hours per DT at the end of 1990.

To analyze these trends in total demand in the residential sector, one must consider the manner in which consumption will be varied by customers over this period. The increase in price of electricity in the long run perhaps would induce trends toward better insulation in houses, heating of selected rooms in the home at different hours, desert air coolers instead of air conditioning, more efficient appliances, and of course a general reduction in the intensity and scale of use of all domestic appliances. In short, in time a new life style could emerge for customers in each rate group that would attempt to reduce demand for electricity. The price effect would be much more significant in the higher rate groups, which would find their present "luxuries" much more expensive, than in the lower rate groups, who use electricity for lighting, refrigeration, and other "necessities." Hence, although the higher consumption groups exhibit a substantial decrease in kilowatt hours per customer by 1990, total residential demand grows in this period due to two effects:

SIMULATION RESULTS

(1) there is a total increase in population in the region, and this results in an absolute increase in the total number of residential customers; and

(2) there is a significant movement of customers from the lower to the higher consumption group. The long run nature of reduction in demand by the higher consumption groups arises out of the possible substitution and change in life style mentioned above, thus making the higher rate structures very attractive to lower rate groups. In simple terms, if the installation of an electric water heater in the home usually requires say, 200 KwH of electricity a month in "normal" use, a customer in the lower rate group may not opt for an electric water heater. If, however, the same customer were to find that the "normal" use of an improved electric water heater is only 50 KwH a month, because everyone (including himself) is using less hot water by substituting deodorant sprays for hot showers, he may decide to install such a heater as it would entitle him to a cheaper rate schedule. Thus, if the current distinction in rates is perpetuated, the percentage of customers in the higher rate groups will increase as the kilowatt hours per customer in these groups keeps falling.

It is relevant to contrast the increase in demand in this sector of up to 14 percent a year witnessed in some recent years with the total increase of 95.6 percent only from mid-1968 to end-1990.

Demand in the Industrial Sector

Prices affecting demand in this sector are in the form of ratios, both for coal versus electricity and fuel oil versus electricity. Again, the assumptions underlying the increase in these price ratios would make the results heavily dependent on those assumptions. Therefore, the forecasts for this sector must be viewed in conjunction with the results of the sensitivity runs involving both a variation in economic growth as well as an increase in prices. For the present, however, this discussion is based on the most likely price assumptions derived from the results of the internal study made available by Carolina Power and Light.

Total employment in all seven industry groups has been assumed to grow linearly, and hence there is a steady increase in the aggregate for the sector starting at a level of 234,000 in mid-1968 to 331,000 in end-1990. This represents an increase of 41.45 percent over the entire period. Total value added by manufacturing industries, however, grows from $0.271 billion to $0.627 billion per DT from the start to the end of the simulation period, which amounts to a 131.37 percent increase. The demand for electricity in terms of kilowatt hours per thousand dollars of value added is 2.904 KwH at the start of the simulated period but increases to 3.87 KwH at the end of 1990. The total demand for electricity in this period, as a result, increases from 787,000 thousand KwH per DT to 2,420,000 thousand KwH. This represents a total increase of 207.49 percent in the period mid-1968 to end-1990. This increase is not uniformly distributed over the entire period. For instance, total demand in the sector would double by the end of 1977, approximately treble by end-1989, and increase further to its end-1990 value. Thus, with the growth assumptions made in this study, demand for electricity will increase by accelerated quantities in the industrial sector. The policy of local and state governments toward industrialization, of course, would have an important impact on these forecasts.

Demand in the Commercial Sector

The three major subgroups in this sector consist of customers in business-related activities, schools or educational institutions, and churches. There are two others which are relatively less important, housing construction and commercial housing. The growth of the number of customers in the former three subgroups has been tabulated and plotted individually as well as the kilowatt hours per customer for each of the five subgroups.

In the business subgroup, the number of customers increases from 60,800 in mid-1968 to 119,000 in end-1990, which amounts to an increase of 95.72 percent. The corresponding values in the schools subgroup are 1,860 and 4,330, respectively, which represents an increase of 132.79 percent. There has been an increase in scale in educational institutions in recent years, which would tend to decrease the number of customers in this subgroup. Thus, the actual increase in customers in recent years and the projected increase up to 1990 can only be explained on the basis that the decrease on account of larger size is being offset by extension of educational and training facilities to sections of the population as yet uninvolved in organized learning activities. There may be some validity in this argument as evidenced by the recent increase in community colleges, evening business institutes, day-care centers, and kindergartens, and of course the general increase in institutions of higher learning. The increase in customers in the church subgroup is slower, rising from 5,380 in mid-1968 to 7,550 by end-1990, a total of 40.33 percent.

SIMULATION RESULTS

Demand per customer in each of these subgroups is as follows in the initial and final periods, respectively:

	Mid-1968 Value (1,000 KwH)	End-1990 Value (1,000 KwH)	Percentage Change
Businesses	5.29	5.44	2.8
Schools	12.0	9.88	-17.7
Churches	1.28	3.07	139.8
Commercial housing	0.893	34.80	3,896
Housing construction	0.23	0.001	-99.56

The above figures may seem abnormal in some respects. The businesses and churches subgroups appear to be stable by comparison with the others. In the schools subgroup, the sharp decline in kilowatt hours per customer admittedly is alarming and perhaps implausible. There could be two reasons for this projected decline.

(1) Since this particular category is often the beneficiary of public funding from various sources, it is possible that its response to price changes and cost considerations cannot be estimated or predicted accurately. In other words, a large increase in prices will not result in a satisfactory reduction in demand but rather could lead to greater public pressure for increased funding to meet the "needs" of the people. Thus, it is possible that the elasticity estimates derived by Halvorsen for the commercial sector as a whole and used in this study greatly exaggerate the long run elasticities for this particular subgroup. A better measure perhaps could be obtained, as specifically related to this category, after a few years when data reflecting response to real price increases as opposed to decreases that have been seen in the past are available. This, then, is an area for further study and investigation and is discussed later in the light of some other assumptions.

(2) If we are to assume that educational institutions respond rationally to prices and costs, then it is possible that the elasticities used in our model are reliable and merely reflect the fact that, faced with larger costs of electricity, these customers will either set up their own generating capacity or change over to new systems eliminating use of electricity; these could be in the nature of heating by gas, oil, or coal, less air conditioning, and more effective insulation in buildings. If this is to be the shape of things to come, planners for the utility concerned should be prepared for lower demand in this subgroup, with the price assumptions used in this part of the simulation runs.

The substantial increase in kilowatt hours per customer in the housing category may not be unreasonable if it were to be perceived that (1) the trend these days is to larger commercial housing due to economies of scale in construction, maintenance, management, landscaping, and so on; and (2) the rates for electricity offered to customers in commercial housing as against residential sector customers are considerably lower. Thus, comparable cost of electricity for a dweller in a commercial housing unit would be much lower than in a residential unit. This would influence the decision of those seeking housing services to the benefit of commercial housing, particularly as electrical costs (which, if rising on a real basis) become a larger fraction of "housing services" costs. There is, therefore, every reason to believe that greater demand and economies of scale will result in the construction of larger commercial housing units in the future, thereby increasing kilowatt hours per customer, as forecast.

Electricity rates for housing construction are high by comparison with other groups in the Carolina Power and Light scheme of pricing. Hence, if for this category rates continue to climb on the same percentage basis as the rest of the commercial sector, quantities of electricity demanded by housing construction customers will almost vanish. This could take place either by utilization of other sources of energy or the organization of mobile supply services, whereby specialized firms or construction agents themselves bring to construction sites small generating units that could supply electricity at cheaper rates than Carolina Power and Light. Overall, the commercial sector will experience a growth in demand from 355,000 thousand KwH in mid-1968 to 1,560,000 thousand KwH by end-1990. This represents an increase of 339.44 percent during this period.

When considering the Carolina Power and Light system as a whole, the aggregate of the residential, industrial, and commercial sectors will exhibit changes as follows:

	Demand in the residential, industrial, and commerical sectors in thousands of kilowatt hours
Mid-1968 Values	1,735,000
Mid-1974 Values	2,760,000
End-1990 Values	5,140,000
Percentage Increase 1968-90	196.25

It can be observed that even though this represents a slowing down of the rate of increase witnessed in the recent past, demand will keep on increasing until 1990, based on the price assumptions used at this stage. It may also be assumed that the resale and street lighting sector not covered by this model will follow the same time path as the aggregate of the three major sectors covered by the study and described above.

SENSITIVITY ANALYSIS

This section deals with an assessment of the sensitivity of certain key variables to changes in certain assumptions driving the dynamic model. The values of the affected variables have been plotted in graphs to bring out the observed differences at a glance. The various simulation runs and results thereof have been arranged as follows:

Variations in Regional Growth

The effects of variation in regional growth assumptions have been analyzed in two ways: first, with the assumption of price increases at the minimum rate projected in the unpublished study cited in Chapter 2, second, at the maximum rate of price increases projected therein. Figures 3.1 to 3.5 give the effect of variations in growth with low price increases. Figures 3.6 and 3.7 show the effect with high price increases.

The graphs lines labeled 1, 2, 3, and 4 on each of Figures 3.1 to 3.5 represent

   1—25 percent higher growth rate than the SCB projection,
   2—growth rate similar to the SCB study,
   3—growth rate 25 percent lower than the SCB projection, and
   4—growth rate 50 percent lower than the SCB projection.

The effects of growth assumptions on the industrial sector have not been investigated, since this effect would be exactly linear on all the industry groups in the model. From observation of the graphs, it would be concluded that the greatest effect of variable growth is on migration and total population applicable to the region. The effects on demand, both in the residential and commercial sectors, also are significant. Overall, therefore, regional growth is an important determinant of demand for electricity.

FIGURE 3.1

Effect of Varying Regional Growth with Low Income per Capita

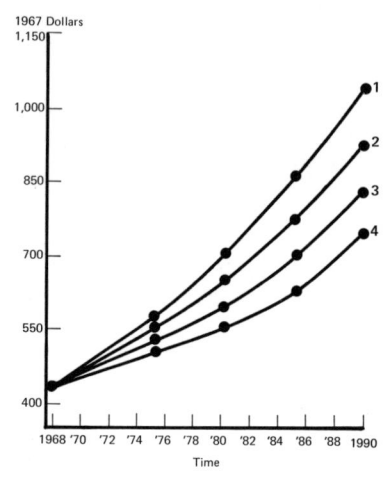

INCOME PER CAPITA

Source: Compiled by author.

FIGURE 3.2

Effect of Varying Regional Growth with Low Electricity Prices on Total Migration

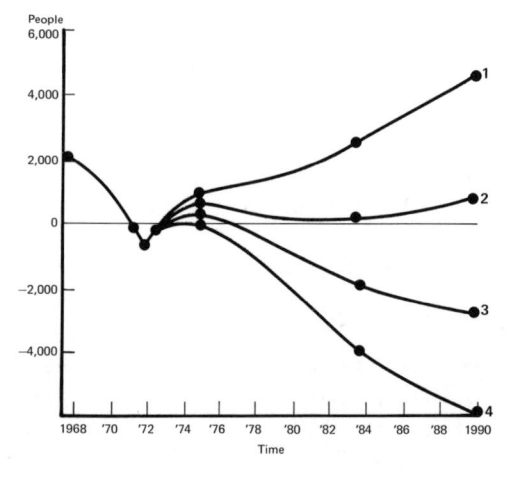

TOTAL MIGRATION

Source: Compiled by author.

FIGURE 3.3

Effect of Varying Regional Growth with Low Electricity Prices on Total Population

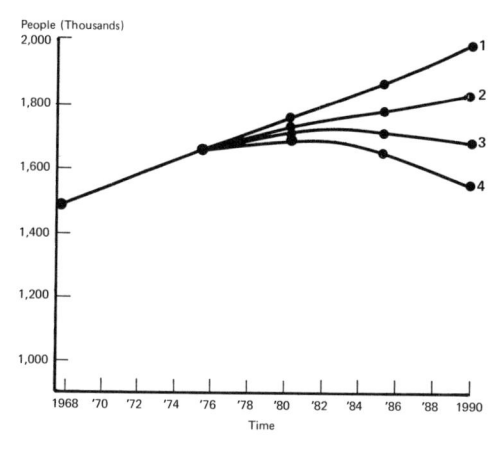

TOTAL POPULATION

Source: Compiled by author.

FIGURE 3.4

Effect of Varying Regional Growth with Low Electricity Prices on Total Demand in Residential Sector

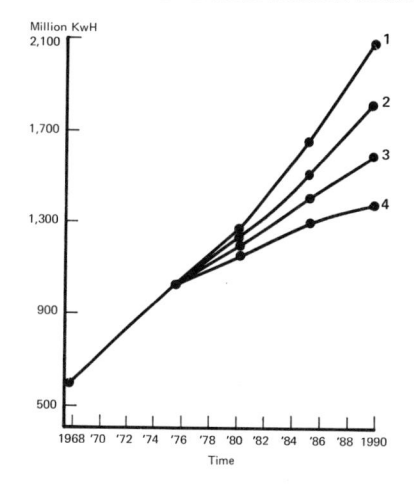

TOTAL DEMAND IN RESIDENTIAL SECTOR

Source: Compiled by author.

FIGURE 3.5

Effect of Varying Regional Growth with Low Electricity Prices
on Total Demand in Commercial Sector

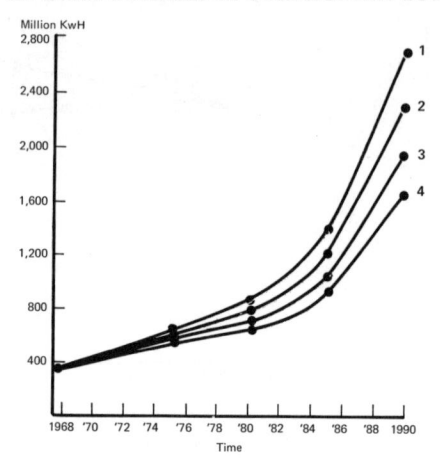

TOTAL DEMAND IN COMMERCIAL SECTOR

Source: Compiled by author.

FIGURE 3.6

Effect of Varying Regional Growth with High Electricity Prices
on Total Demand in Residential Sector

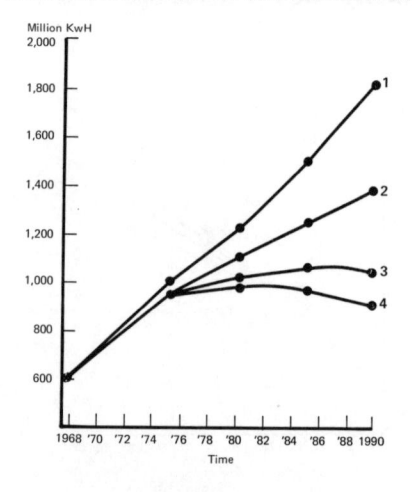

DEMAND IN RESIDENTIAL SECTOR

Source: Compiled by author.

SIMULATION RESULTS 71

FIGURE 3.7

Effect of Varying Regional Growth with High Electricity Prices
on Total Demand in Commercial Sector

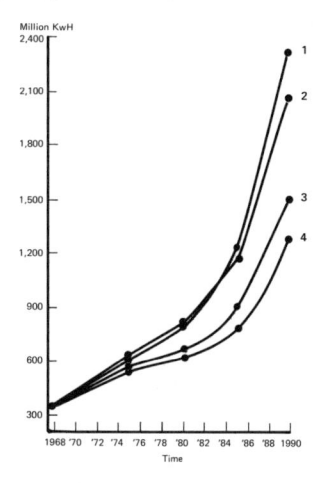

DEMAND IN COMMERCIAL SECTOR

Source: Compiled by author.

In Figures 3.6 to 3.7, the effect of different rates of economic growth on demand for electricity in two sectors—residential and commercial—has been graphed.

An examination of Figures 3.1 and 3.2 in comparison with Figures 3.4 and 3.5 shows that the divergence in values with the four different growth assumptions is much greater for Figures 3.1 and 3.2 than for Figures 3.4 and 3.5. In fact with Figure 3.4, assuming a growth rate 50 percent lower than the SCB study, residential sector demand actually starts declining beyond period 76, that is, beyond 1980. The effect on demand in the commercial sector is, however, not as pronounced as on the residential sector. Thus, a combination of low rates of economic growth and high increases in real electricity prices would have the greatest effect on the validity of forecasts pertaining to the residential sector.

Variations in National Growth

In this section the growth assumptions for the region have been held constant in accordance with the SCB study, but the rate of growth of U.S. per capita income has been varied at (1) 25 percent above the

72   ELECTRICAL SUPPLY AND DEMAND

projected rate and (2) 25 percent below the SCB projected rate. Values for different variables have been plotted as graph lines 1 and 2 in each case in accordance with the above two assumptions. These are shown as Figures 3.8 to 3.12.

The effect of these assumptions is felt strongly on values for migration and total population, as can be seen in Figures 3.9 and 3.10. Consequently, the effect on demand in the residential sector is greater than on the commercial sector, as can be seen in Figures 3.11 and 3.12. Again, since the effect would be exactly linear, no explicit attempt was made to test these effects on the industrial sector.

FIGURE 3.8

Effect of Varying National Growth
on U.S. per Capita Income

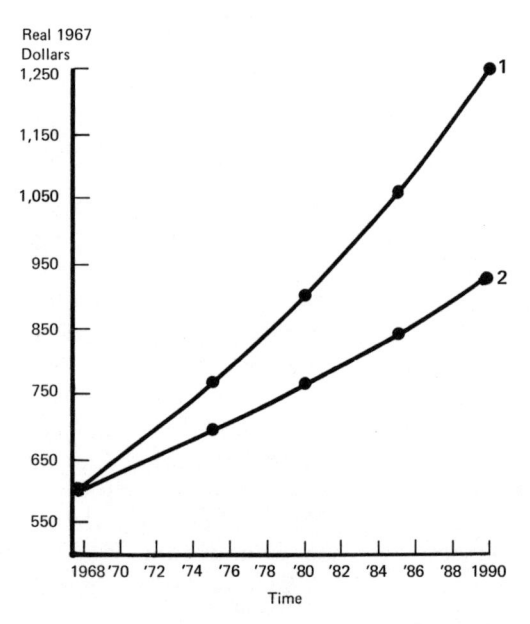

U.S. PER CAPITA INCOME

Source: Compiled by author.

FIGURE 3.9

Effect of Varying National Growth
on Regional Migration

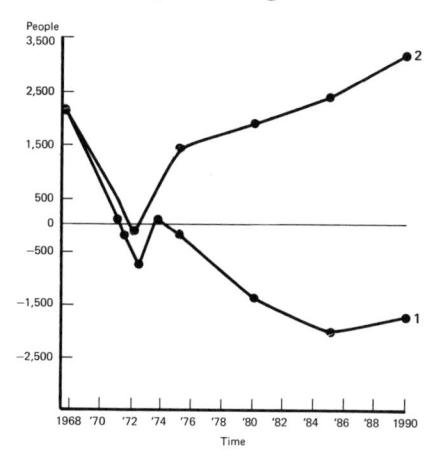

TOTAL MIGRATION

Source: Compiled by author.

FIGURE 3.10

Effect of Varying National Growth
on Regional Population

TOTAL POPULATION

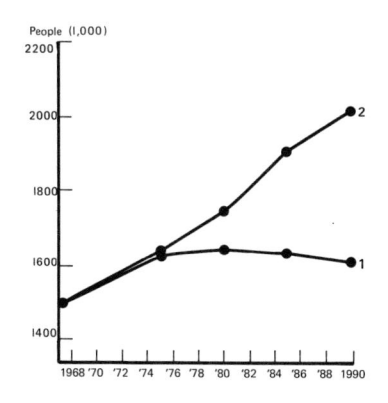

Source: Compiled by author.

FIGURE 3.11

Effect of Varying National Growth
on Total Demand in Residential Sector

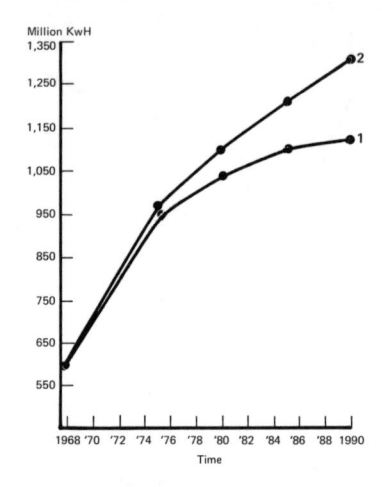

DEMAND IN RESIDENTIAL SECTOR

Source: Compiled by author.

FIGURE 3.12

Effect of Varying National Growth
on Total Demand in Commercial Sector

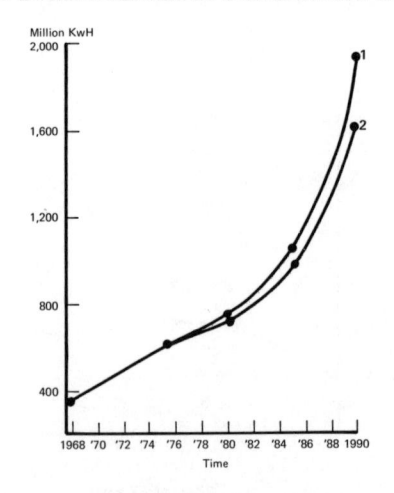

DEMAND IN COMMERCIAL SECTOR

Source: Compiled by author.

SIMULATION RESULTS

Variations in Increase in Electricity Prices

In this set of simulation runs, the effect of different rates of price increases were tested in relation to demand in each of the three sectors. The assumptions used for simulation were

(1) all prices, including electricity, fuel oil, coal, and gas, growing at a two-month rate of 0.9 percent;

(2) all other prices growing at the highest rate given in the study, except electricity prices, which grow at 25 percent lower than the high price increase rate (0.675 percent for electricity, 0.9 percent for coal, 1.7 percent for gas and fuel oil);

(3) all other prices growing at the highest rate except electricity prices, which grow at 25 percent greater than the probable rate (that is, 0.1.125 percent); and

(4) all prices growing at the highest rate (coal and electricity 0.9 percent, natural gas and fuel oil 1.7 percent).

Figures 3.13 to 3.15 show the effects of these variations in prices. In this case it will be observed that the greatest effect is on demand

FIGURE 3.13

Effect of Varying Prices on Total Demand in Residential Sector

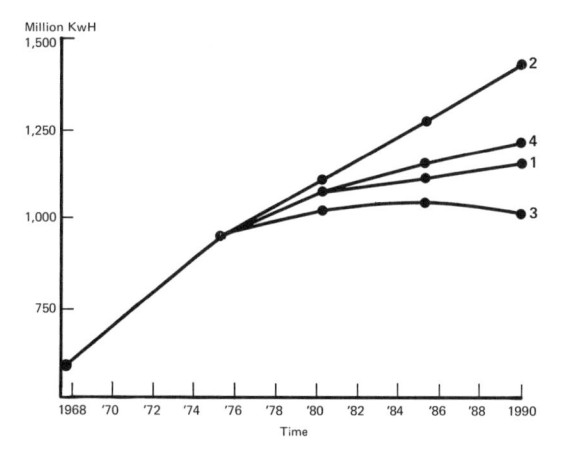

TOTAL DEMAND IN RESIDENTIAL SECTOR

Source: Compiled by author.

FIGURE 3.14

Effect of Varying Prices on Total Demand
in Commercial Sector

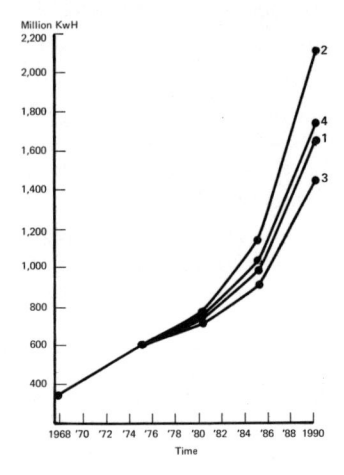

TOTAL DEMAND IN COMMERCIAL SECTOR

Source: Compiled by author.

FIGURE 3.15

Effect of Varying Prices on Total Demand
in Industrial Sector

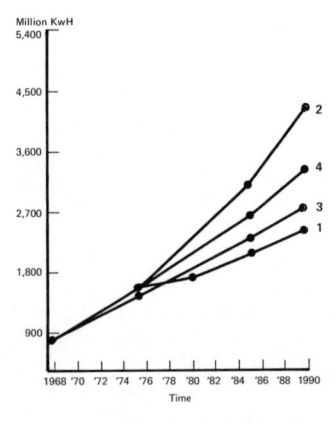

TOTAL DEMAND IN INDUSTRIAL SECTOR

Source: Compiled by author.

SIMULATION RESULTS

in the industrial sector, although almost equally great on the residential sector. The effect on the commercial sector is comparatively more stable.

Variations in Rate of Change of Average Household Size

Two simulation runs were carried out using a 25 percent higher rate of change of household size and a 25 percent lower rate of change of household size than the adopted normal for the region. Results have not been graphed because they reveal a relationship as expected, showing a negative effect of household size on demand in the residential sector.

From a broad assessment of the results obtained above it is clear that economic variables and increase in electricity prices will have the greatest effect on demand in the residential sector and a surprisingly small effect on the aggregate commercial sector demand. Thus pricing policies may be directed to stabilize demand in the residential sector, should the utility desire to offset the effects of changes in economic variables in the future. Similar efforts in pricing policies for the commercial sector may not bear adequate returns. These options are examined in greater detail later in Part II to determine what pricing policies must be adopted by the utilities and regulating agencies to ensure that demand will be met fully in the years ahead. These prices, of course, would be determined as a result of the utility's existing financial position, and attempts would be made to balance the firm's profit-earning objectives with the problems of supply and demand as they apply to the specific region served by it.

Up to this point the book has concentrated on developing a suitable model for the utility's demand function to use it as the basis for development of policy alternatives. Such policy investigations will be attempted after a treatment of the supply of electrical energy is presented in Part II.

PART II
THE SUPPLY OF ELECTRICAL ENERGY

INTRODUCTION TO PART II

The supply of electrical energy embraces three distinct functions—generation, transmission, and distribution. Whereas the specific generating technology adopted in practice is, to a large degree, independent of the distances and geographic dispersal of potential customers, transmission and distribution systems are locked intimately into the spatial characteristics of the consumption point to be served. The choices available between alternative power generation methods consequently are more numerous and distinct than those for transmission and distribution. A discussion of the choices in generation, therefore, is much more relevant to the dynamics of the electrical energy sector and has been given prominence in Part II. This is not to say that the economics of transmission and distribution are of no concern in utilitywide or national plans. In fact, transmission and distribution costs are a major part of the costs incurred by investor-owned electric utilities, both in construction and operation. The Federal Power Commission (FPC)[1] predicts a steady decline in the share of transmission and distribution costs, as a percentage of the total, over the next few decades. Table II.1 shows these percentages for the entire United States for 1962, 1968, and the FPC's projections for 1990.

TABLE II.1

Percentage Breakdown of Costs of Electricity Supplied in the United States

	1962	1968	1972[*]	1990 (Projected)
Generation	51	50	59.2	60
Transmission	9.9	13	13.1	16
Distribution	39.1	37	23.0	24
Total	100	100	95.3	100

[*]Computed from Edison Electric Institute statistics for construction expenditures only. Balance is under the heading of other costs.

Source: Federal Power Commission. The 1970 National Power Survey (Washington, D.C.: Government Printing Office, 1971), p. II-39.

TABLE II.2

Construction Expenditures—Investor-Owned Electric Utilities
Excluding Alaska and Hawaii
by type of electric utility plant
millions of dollars

Year	Total	Production	Transmission	Distribution	Other
1973	14,907	8,775	2,047	3,371	714
1972	13,385	7,931	1,748	3,073	633
1971	11,894	6,702	1,806	2,774	612
1970	10,145	5,429	1,680	2,614	422
1969	8,294	3,992	1,554	2,421	327
1968	7,140	3,189	1,503	2,135	313
1967	6,120	2,553	1,323	1,977	267
1966	4,932	1,789	1,137	1,769	237
1965	4,027	1,300	940	1,585	202
1964	3,551	1,114	824	1,424	189
1963	3,319	1,165	644	1,323	187
1962	3,154	1,078	609	1,305	162
1961	3,256	1,267	579	1,265	145
1960	3,331	1,342	537	1,300	152
1959	3,383	1,519	554	1,163	147
1958	3,764	1,879	608	1,125	152
1957	3,679	1,647	594	1,270	168
1956	2,910	1,029	455	1,274	152
1955	2,719	1,064	434	1,093	128
1954	2,835	1,280	464	993	98
1953	2,876	1,391	442	938	105
1952	2,599	1,251	379	879	90
1951	2,134	920	300	810	104

Source: Edison Electric Institute, Statistical Year Book of the Electric Utility Industry for 1973 (New York: Edison Electric Institute, 1974), p. 59.

The actual expenditures incurred in millions of dollars year by year in the form of generation, distribution, and transmission and other costs for all investor-owned U.S. utilities for the period 1951-73 are shown in Table II.2.

These figures support the observation that for a geographic region highly saturated with the supply of electricity, generating costs increase more rapidly than those incurred directly in transmission and distribution. Further, in the foreseeable future, the

INTRODUCTION TO PART II

inputs required in power generation are those that may impose constraints on growth both by way of large price increases and temporary physical shortages as a result of this country's dependence on imports of crude oil and possibly nuclear fuels. The concern of most U.S. electric utilities today, as well as that of the federal and state governments, relates mainly to augmentation of generating capacity to satisfy anticipated increases in demand. The focus in Part II, therefore, has been limited to an exposition of the various economic factors that influence the generation of electricity. Since such a treatment necessarily has to be general, frequent references to the Carolina Power and Light system in particular have been avoided. Before the economic and financial aspects of electricity supply are explored in detail, a discussion of some technical developments in power generation is presented in Chapter 4.

NOTE

1. Federal Power Commission, The 1970 National Power Survey (Washington, D.C.: Government Printing Office, 1971), p. II-34.

CHAPTER

4

POWER GENERATION ALTERNATIVES

Hydroelectric Generation

The construction and operation of hydroelectric plants in the United States still has a great deal of potential. The Federal Power Commission (FPC), which maintains a record of developed and undeveloped hydroelectric power capacity in the country, reported that on January 1, 1972, the United States had hydroelectric generating potential of 178.6 million Kw capable of yielding 702 billion KwH annually[1] Of this potential, approximately 53.4 million Kw, or 30 percent of the total, had been developed providing a total capability of 257 billion KwH annually; and about 7.8 million Kw were under construction on that date. Since the 1930s, the United States has witnessed a fivefold increase in total installed hydropower capacity; but this increase has been dwarfed by a much faster growth in steam-electric capacity, particularly in the last two decades.

A distinct feature of hydroelectric power generation is the absence of any fuel in the process. Essentially the "fuel" used by this method is the energy from the sun, which is responsible for the cycles or rainfall, runoff, evaporation, and transpiration. Hydroelectric plants do not consume water; nor do they cause thermal and air pollution, which usually accompany the operation of thermal plants. However, environmentalists often object to hydroelectric projects on the grounds that the nation's most beautiful gorges and river valleys are converted into large, monotonous lakes. Also, certain fishes of commercial and recreational interest, such as salmon, are often completely eliminated by the development of such projects. On the other hand, some recreational activities, such as power boating, water skiing, and warm-water fishing are created by the presence of a large lake.

Hydroelectric plants utilize flowing water to produce electrical energy by turbine-generator sets. The flowing water imparts kinetic energy to a turbine wheel, which in turn drives a generator coupled to it. The rate of production of hydroelectric energy is limited by the flow rate and pressure head of water driving the plant. An adequate flow rate can be ensured by the formation of a large lake or reservoir. However, the topography of a suitable project site must not only permit the filling up of a large enough reservoir volume but also provide the necessary pressure head for the flowing water to develop the required velocity under the effect of gravity.

In the United States, the Pacific northwest region has been endowed generously with a number of suitable hydropower sites. But, climatic factors in that part of the country result in a greater demand for electrical energy in the winter months as against the rest, necessitating dams and a large storage capacity to collect water from melting snow and rain in other months for enhanced flow and power generation during the winter. Thus, in a sense, hydroelectric projects are capable of storing energy in periods of lean demand.

The Carolinas are not endowed geographically with an abundance of hydroelectric potential. As such, Carolina Power and Light Company operates four separate hydroelectric plants with a total capacity of 219,600 Kw and had average annual generation of 894.8 million KwH of electrical energy in 1973. The largest of these has an installed capacity of 108,000 Kw, but the other three have capacities of less than 100,000 Kw, respectively. Small capacity plants usually have no upstream storage capacity and must use water at the same rate at which it enters the reservoir. Otherwise, all or part of it would have to be spilled past the plant, losing the energy carried in the water. Such plants are usually known as run-of-the-river type.

Plants with adequate storage capacity upstream can be constructed for use in conjunction with downstream run-of-the-river plants. The upstream storage in such a case serves the downstream plants also when the operation of all plants is coordinated with the quantity of water released for generation from the reservoir. By this process, the energy from the water is extracted to the fullest extent to serve a seasonally fluctuating demand for electrical energy. Figure 4.1 shows three different plants, A, B, and C, located on a river such that A has large storage capacity, B somewhat less, and C very limited storage. The large reservoir of plant A permits a great deal of flexibility in operation; water can be collected and held in the reservoir with a small discharge during periods of low electricity demand. Plants B and C have, progressively, less flexibility and take up the work of regular base load operation on a continuous basis.

A simplified schedule of load sharing between A, B, and C for different hours in the day is shown in Figure 4.2.

FIGURE 4.1

Distribution of Storage Capacity Between
Different Plants in Series

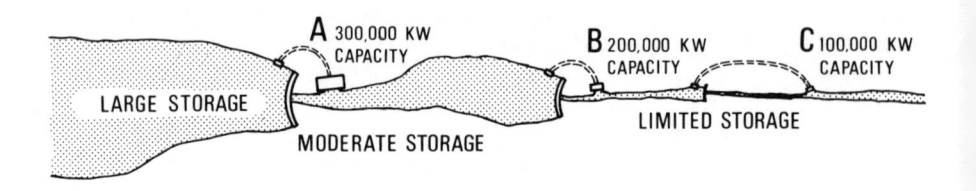

Source: Courtesy Messrs. Cone-Heiden

FIGURE 4.2

Load Sharing between Plants on the Same River

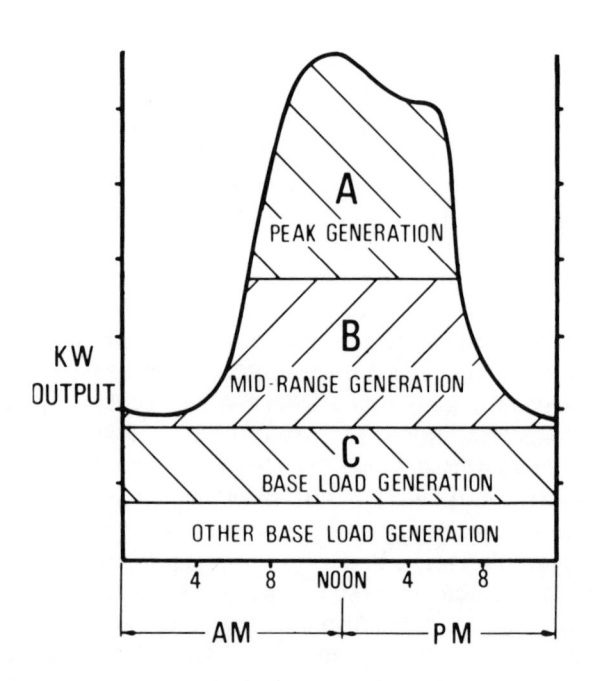

Source: Courtesy Messrs. Cone-Heiden

POWER GENERATION ALTERNATIVES   87

This example shows how the maximum possible energy available in the water can be extracted with the storage of energy in a large upstream reservoir. If required, the three plants could be working simultaneously to deliver a uniform base load where no fluctuations in demand exist. Another possibility, which may require higher capital costs, would be to install A, B, and C with the same generating capacity and to use all three for peak load generation, with controlled fluctuations in the flow of water discharged. However, these alternatives necessarily may not result in an increase in the annual energy produced by the three plants. The only means for extracting a larger amount of energy from the water would be by construction of additional plants either upstream or downstream. Naturally, with a given set of geographic characteristics, the establishment of hydroelectric plants beyond a certain number and aggregate capacity would prove uneconomical. Some figures representing construction and operating costs will be provided in Chapter 5, but it would be relevant to observe here that some of the economic advantages of hydroelectric power generation are low operating charges and no fuel costs. Maintenance costs are low since the machinery involved is simple and robust. Interruption of supply is unlikely; and such plants are capable of a "black start," that is, no external source is required to start the turbines. However, since the plant location is constrained to specific geographic sites, transmission lines usually are extensive. Hence, transmission costs usually are much higher than for thermal plants.

Technical developments in hydroelectric generation have been impressive in the 1960s and 1970s. European designs for turbines are now capable of developing the economic potential of sites that physically permit pressure heads of as low as 10 to 15 feet. Developments such as these, accompanied by rising costs of alternative methods, could spur a period of increased hydroelectric construction in the future. This, however, is unlikely to reverse the trend of a smaller percentage of power generation by hydroelectric plants. Thus far, little work has been done in studying the tremendous hydroelectrical potential available in Alaska, which may be also developed in the future. Increasing imports from hydroelectric sources in Canada are also a possibility. With all these factors accounted for, the FPC[2] estimated an increase in hydroelectric generating capacity to about 82,000 Mw (megawatts) by 1990.

Conventional Steam-Powered Generation

The largest share of electricity generated in this country is provided by conventional steam plants, estimated in 1972 to be 80.9 percent. Against this, the Carolina Power and Light system in 1973 operated a total of 79 percent in its conventional steam plants, of which the coal-fired plants provided 67 percent and residual oil 12 percent.

The different components of a steam-powered plant are similar, even for the different fossil fuels widely used in producing steam. These are mainly the boiler, fuel storage and handling equipment, steam turbine coupled with electric generator, air pollution control equipment, condenser and pumps, and fans and heaters. There are, nevertheless, differences in boiler design, fule preparation, and pollution control equipment, depending on the fuel for which a particular plant is designed. Some plants are designed for burning either coal or fuel oil to provide greater flexibility in fuel supply. Both natural gas-fired and oil-fired plants require no electrostatic precipators for removal of particulate matter. The particulate matter formed by combustion in these plants is within current standards laid down by the Environmental Protection Agency and requires no removal. In coal-based plants some pulverized coal does not burn completely, leaving residual ash as much as 16 percent of the total weight of the coal used, which requires mandatory use of electrostatic precipitators.

Another environmental problem encountered in coal and oil-based plants is the emission of sulfur dioxide gas, which can be controlled most effectively by the use of high grade, low sulfur fuels only. Oxides of nitrogen are also formed as a by-product of combustion of all hydrocarbons or coal, and in power plants this reaction can be reduced by lowering boiler temperatures. But this leads to a reduction in thermal efficiency.

The total thermal efficiency for most steam-powered plants is between 35 to 41 percent. Of the total energy released by combusion of the fuel, part of it is carried away to the atmosphere by the products of combustion, part is lost by radiation, convection, and conduction to the surroundings; and the remainder is imparted to the steam used for driving the turbine. Here again only a part of the energy available in the steam is converted into mechanical energy by the turbine, and a part of this is converted into electrical energy by the generator. The thermal efficiency of U.S. steam-powered plants has improved significantly, but no major improvements are expected in the near future. Recent trends can be seen from the following U.S. figures estimated by the Edison Electric Institute for all fossil fuels used in power generation.[3] The dramatic improvement reflected in these figures for the period 1951-60 was actually brought about by the development of plants using steam at super critical pressures of 3,500 to 5,000 pounds per square inch and temperatures of 1,100 to 1,200 degrees.

In a publication by the City of Seattle[4], the authors have calculated the amounts of fuel used and by-products produced for a typical 1-million Kw plant using three fuels: coal, oil, and gas, respectively.

POWER GENERATION ALTERNATIVES 89

Year	Thermal Efficiency in Btu per KwH
1973	10,409
1972	10,479
1969	10,457
1966	10,399
1963	10,438
1960	10,701
1957	11,365
1954	12,180
1951	13,641

Figure 4.3

Coal-Fired Plant Mass Balance

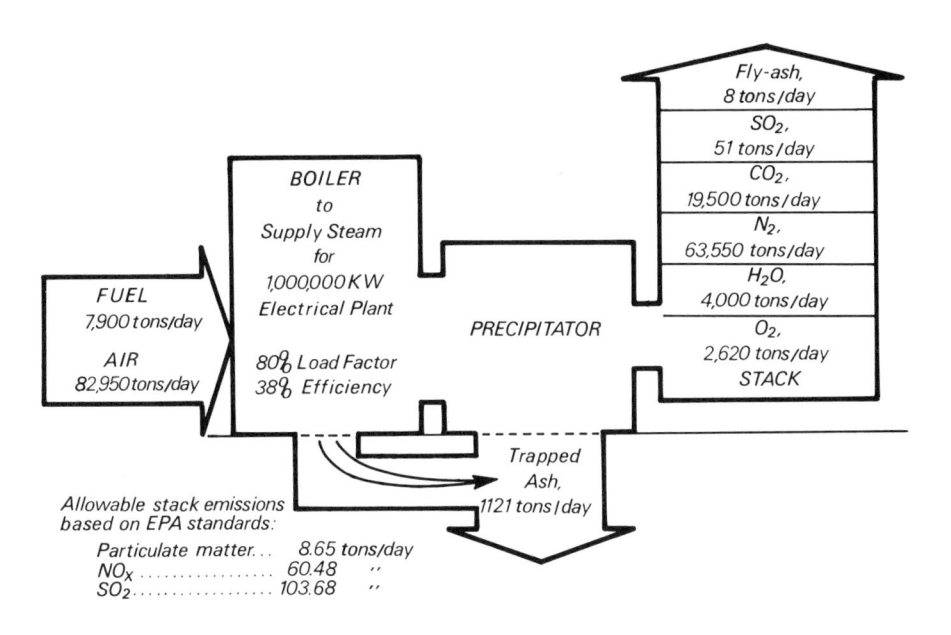

FUEL 7,900 tons/day
AIR 82,950 tons/day

BOILER to Supply Steam for 1,000,000 KW Electrical Plant
80% Load Factor
38% Efficiency

PRECIPITATOR

Fly-ash, 8 tons/day
SO_2, 51 tons/day
CO_2, 19,500 tons/day
N_2, 63,550 tons/day
H_2O, 4,000 tons/day
O_2, 2,620 tons/day
STACK

Trapped Ash, 1121 tons/day

Allowable stack emissions based on EPA standards:
Particulate matter... 8.65 tons/day
NO_x .... 60.48 ''
SO_2 .... 103.68 ''

Source: Courtesy Messrs. Cone-Heiden.

Assuming 38 percent thermal efficiency for all three plants, the mass balance for operation of each was presented, which is shown in Figures 4.3 to 4.5.

The quantities shown above bring out the importance of efficient transportation in feeding the plant with the requisite tonnage of coal. Wherever the distances of plants from coal mines are large, costs

FIGURE 4.4

Oil-Fired Plant Mass Balance

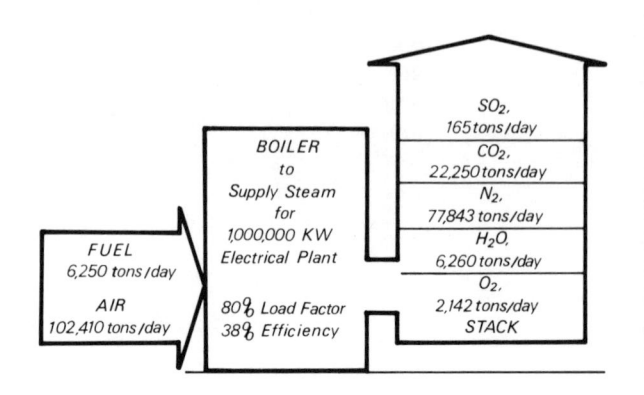

```
                    ┌─────────────┐
                    │   BOILER    │   SO₂,
                    │     to      │   165 tons/day
                    │ Supply Steam│   CO₂,
                    │     for     │   22,250 tons/day
   FUEL             │ 1,000,000 KW│   N₂,
   6,250 tons/day ──│  Electrical │   77,843 tons/day
                    │    Plant    │   H₂O,
   AIR              │             │   6,260 tons/day
   102,410 tons/day │ 80% Load    │   O₂,
                    │   Factor    │   2,142 tons/day
                    │ 38% Efficiency│  STACK
                    └─────────────┘
```

Allowable stack emissions
based on EPA standards:
  Particulate matter... 8.65 tons/day
  NO$_x$ .... 25.92   "
  SO$_2$ .... 69.12   "

Source: Courtesy Messrs. Cone-Heiden.

of transportation would be substantial. The by-products that would require disposal are indicated in the figure, but the quantity of NO$_x$ (oxides of nitrogen) produced would depend on furnace temperatures. To meet current Environmental Protection Agency (EPA) standards, boilers installed in the future will have to be redesigned for lower temperatures, thereby leading to a slightly lower thermal efficiency.

With the oil-fired plant, the balance shown in Figure 4.4 indicates 165 tons of SO$_2$ (sulfur dioxide) discharge with an input of high sulfur oil. This exceeds the current EPA limits, which can be adhered to by using low sulfur oil, but the changeover would result in an increase in fuel costs. The amount of NO$_x$ produced would depend, as before, on the design of the boiler combustion space.

With a 1-million Kw gas-fired plant there will be no SO$_2$ discharge because natural gas contains only traces of sulfur. The problem of NO$_x$ formation, however, exists in this case also and can be alleviated by reduction in boiler temperatures at a loss of thermal efficiency.

In addition to the above features, fossil-fuel based plants require voluminous supplies of water for cooling the steam condensers. In most cases cooling towers or spray ponds may be used for such cooling processes, but this has the undesirable effect of building up a fog

POWER GENERATION ALTERNATIVES   91

FIGURE 4.5

Gas-Fired Plant Mass Balance

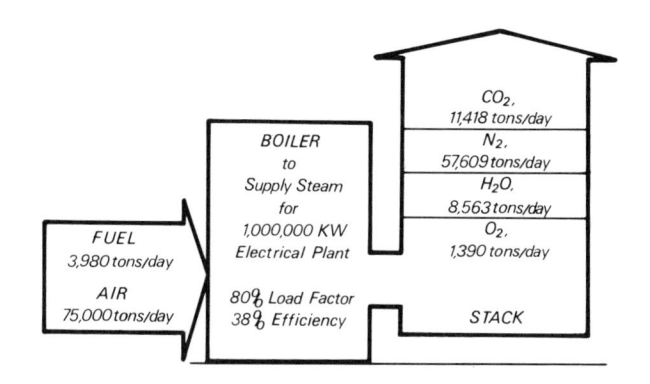

```
                                            ┌─────────────┐
                                            │    CO₂,     │
                                            │ 11,418 tons/day │
                               ┌──────────┐ ├─────────────┤
                               │  BOILER  │ │     N₂,     │
                               │    to    │ │ 57,609 tons/day │
                               │Supply Steam│ ├─────────────┤
                               │   for    │ │    H₂O,     │
                    FUEL       │1,000,000 KW│ │ 8,563 tons/day │
                 3,980 tons/day│Electrical Plant│ ├─────────────┤
                               │          │ │    O₂,      │
                    AIR        │          │ │ 1,390 tons/day │
                 75,000 tons/day│80% Load Factor│ ├─────────────┤
                               │38% Efficiency│ │   STACK     │
                               └──────────┘ └─────────────┘
```

Allowable stack emissions based on EPA standards:
  Particulate matter.... 8.65 tons/day
  NO$_x$ .... 17.28   "
  SO$_2$ ...Sulphur content of fuel negligible

Source: Courtesy Messrs. Cone-Heiden.

in the surrounding atmosphere. Dry cooling towers can be used as a substitute, but the heat dissipation area required in designing them increases their costs substantially. Coal-fired plants require relatively more routine maintenance and cleaning on account of the large amount of ash produced during combustion. The initial investment required in coal based plants is also somewhat higher due to the extra coal handling, storage, pulverizing, and ash disposal equipment required. Fuel oil, on the other hand, requires heating during storage to prevent it from thickening and clogging the feed pipes, and this item requires a slightly higher expenditure. The economics of generation using alternative means are discussed in Chapter 5; at this stage some of the technical and operational features have been described to give the reader some insight into what factors contribute to differences in investment and operation costs.

INTERNAL COMBUSTION TURBINE GENERATION

Another alternative used in power generation employs internal combustion turbines fired by natural gas as well as fuel oils. This process is based on two stages—the first requiring the burning of hydrocarbon fuel in a combustion chamber into which both the fuel and compressed air are admitted and ignited; the second stage requires the burned gas, which develops very high pressure, to be fed into the turbine stage and finally emitted into the atmosphere. The advantage of an internal combustion turbine generator lies in its compact design, rapid cold starting characteristics, and the ability to reach full load generation without long waiting periods. Each turbine usually develops 25,000 to 50,000 Kw and, as such, a typical plant uses a battery of them to develop higher ranges of power. In 1973, Carolina Power and Light generated 2.5 percent of its total energy supplied by internal combustion turbines, but in 1974 it commissioned a new 630,000-Kw plant utilizing 11 internal combustion generating units. It is interesting to note that in 1973, even though the share of energy supplied by internal combustion plants was only 2.5 percent of the total, the capability of these plants represented 10.4 percent of the total Carolina Power and Light-owned 5,364,400-Kw capacity. This indicates that the utility used these plants mainly for satisfying peak demand. Relatively low investment costs and maintenance, as well as easy cold starting qualities, make internal combustion plants an attractive alternative for intermittent peaking operation. Thermal efficiencies for these plants are usually below 30 percent but can be increased by using the hot exhaust gases from the turbine for preheating the air used in combustion. The noise level from modern internal combustion turbines is low enough to make them acceptable for siting even in residential areas, which is usually not possible with conventional steam-powered plants.

NUCLEAR POWER GENERATION

Nuclear power generation is the fastest growing element in the supply of electrical energy today. Nuclear reactors used in power generation are based on nuclear fission and are usually light water reactors (LWR) of either the boiling water reactor (BWR) type or the pressurized water reactor (PWR) type.

A brief discussion of the scientific principles underlying nuclear power generation would be relevant. A diagram of the nuclear plant system is shown in Figure 4.6. The energy source in this system is

POWER GENERATION ALTERNATIVES

FIGURE 4.6

Single-Cycle Reactor System

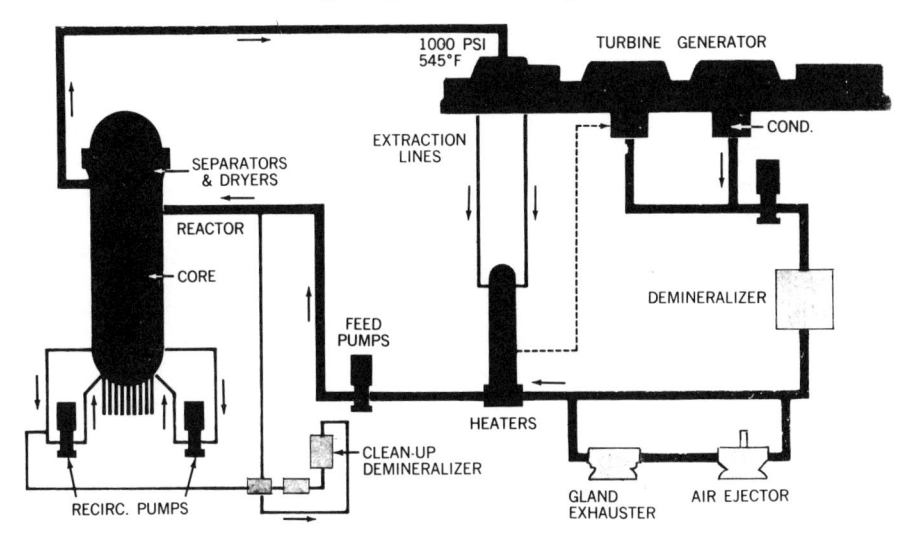

Source: Courtesy Messrs. Cone-Heiden and General Electric Company.

the reactor core itself, in which controlled nuclear fission takes place. The energy produced in fission is in accordance with Einstein's formula

$$E = mc^2$$

where E is energy in ergs, m is the relevant mass in grams, and c is the velocity of light (expressed as 2.998×10^{10} centimeters per second). Nuclear fission takes place when an atom of fissionable material is bombarded by a neutron, bringing about splitting of the atom to release more neutrons, which in turn bombard other atoms. The mass of an atom before fission is much larger than after it, and the difference between the two masses is equivalent to the large release of energy given by the above equation. This large conversion ratio between matter and energy can be visualized from the fact that one pound of fissionable material can produce approximately the energy obtainable from 1,400 tons of coal.

Not all materials are fissionable; uranium-235 is the only naturally occurring material that can be directly used in fission. However, U-235 is available only to the extent of 0.7 percent in naturally mined uranium, the balance consisting mainly of U-238. Other fissionable materials are U-233 and plutonium-239, which can be produced from U-238 and thorium-232, respectively.

Reactors that are in use currently are the thermal or slow type. Uranium-238, which is present in the fuel used in such reactors, has the property of absorbing neutrons, which have greater kinetic energy than the atoms of the core material. This adsorption brings about a reduction in the neutrons available for fission, and hence the speed of neutrons has to be reduced to diminish the adsorptive power of the U-238 atoms. This slowing down is brought about by collision with atoms of a moderator material, which have the property of reducing neutron speed without absorbing a large amount of the neutrons themselves.

Efficiency in using fuel requires that as many of the released neutrons as possible bombard the fissionable atoms. A measure of the efficient continuance of the nuclear reaction is provided by the number of neutrons emitted from every neutron that is absorbed by the fuel. Table 4.1 gives the average figures for this measure for different types of nuclear fuels.

Only one neutron is necessary for maintaining the chain reaction, and the balance number released can be used for converting U-238 or thorium-232 into fissionable material. When such a process is carried out, it is known as breeding. Fast breeder reactors are still under development, and in the United States generation of electricity from breeder reactors on a commercial scale is not likely to take place before the 1980s. The future development of electricity from breeder reactors is discussed in the following chapters.

Of the different types of reactors currently employed, BWR use water boiled in the reactor core directly for driving the steam turbine generator. Shielding the entire steam system is necessary while operating such plants, since the steam carries some radioactivity. The water cycle in a BWR is a closed one; the steam exhausted from the turbines is condensed and pumped back to the core for reheating, while the cooling water circulated in the condenser is pumped to a cooling tower or lake to dissipate the heat collected by it.

The reactor core itself can be of different forms. The most common type uses zircaloy-coated fuel bars containing uranium oxide with low enriched uranium, along with a series of control rods and in-core flux monitors. Fission is controlled by the arrangement of these bars, producing the required range of heat for producing steam. The BWR is essentially a self-regulating reactor because an increase in production of steam causes neutron speed to increase, which in turn reduces the proportion of atoms bombarded for the nuclear chain reaction and hence the rate of heat energy produced reduces.

TABLE 4.1

Average Number of Neutrons Emitted per
Neutron Absorbed by the Fuel

	U-233	U-235	PU-239	Natural Uranium
Thermal neutrons	2.27	2.06	2.10	1.33
Fast neutrons	2.60	2.18	2.74	1.09

Source: Samuel Glasstone and Alexander Sesonoke, Nuclear Reactor Engineering (Princeton: Von Nostrand, 1963), p. 154.

On the other hand, PWR use two coolant loops in the system. In the main or primary loop, pressurized water is pumped through the reactor to extract the heat produced in the reactor. It is then sent through the secondary loop, wherein the heated water transfers its heat in a steam generator to the secondary water, producing steam. This arrangement eliminates the presence of radioactivity in the resultant steam, as is found in the case of the BWR system. The steam is then used for driving a turbine generator, and the exhaust is again cooled as in the BWR and pumped back to the steam generator in keeping with a closed cycle. The PWR core is constructed somewhat differently from the BWR core. Also, since no steam is produced in the primary loop, boric acid initially is added to the primary water to moderate the nuclear reaction.

The thermal efficiency of LWR plants of the two types described above is between 30 to 33 percent, which is lower than conventional steam plants. The scale of turbines, generators, and other equipment used in a nuclear plant is larger than in a conventional steam plant since the former uses steam at lower temperatures and pressures. Nuclear plants also require larger cooling towers since a greater proportion of the heat remains unutilized in the turbine exhaust. Cooling can sometimes be achieved by using a large body of natural water such as a lake, but this would be feasible only in some sites, and environmental concerns are opposing strongly the use of lakes and ponds for cooling purposes. The large Harris plant currently being built by Carolina Power and Light in North Carolina, recently has been subjected to a design change requiring the provision of cooling towers instead of the use of a large lake in which normal water temperatures were estimated to go up by not more than 6 degrees when the plant went into full operation. This change was preceded by a lively debate at the local and state levels, during which

96　　　　　　　　　　ELECTRICAL SUPPLY AND DEMAND

diverse groups of concerned citizens banded together to oppose the use of the lake situated in Wake County as a cooling facility for the Harris plant.

Another area of public concern is the handling and disposal of nuclear fuel. The handling system for a LWR ensures complete safety in handling and storage from receipt of new fuel at site to shipping of used fuel. The reactor refueling arrangement withdraws vertically all the spent fuel from the core and moves it to a special machine that stores it underwater, in safety against the hazard of possible radiation. After a few weeks it is dispatched in sealed containers to a reprocessing plant. A great deal of automation and complex instrumentation is provided for control of the fuel handling arrangements.

Another form of reactor used is a high temperature, gas-cooled reactor (HTGR), which pressurizes a gas, such as helium, circulating through the core and produces steam in the steam generators. On account of the superheating of steam possible in this plant, turbines are operated at three different stages to extract as much energy as possible from the steam. The prestressed concrete reactor vessel (PCRV) system in this plant houses the steam generators and helium circulators. A schematic diagram of a typical HTGR is shown in Figure 4.7.

FIGURE 4.7

Schematic Flow Diagram of High-Temperature
Gas-Cooled Reactor Plant

SCHEMATIC FLOW DIAGRAM

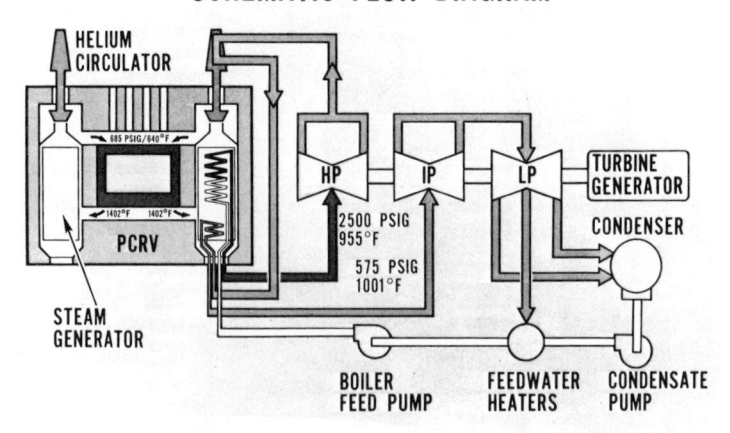

Source: Courtesy Messrs. Cone-Heiden and Gulf General Atomic.

An improved version of the HTGR is still under development that would eliminate the use of steam in driving the turbines and instead would use a set of gas turbines. In addition, this would eliminate much auxiliary equipment, such as the steam condenser, and reduce the size of the turbines, which are much more compact in the case of gas. Consequently, capital costs associated with HTGR plants are expected to be much lower than for present LWR plants.

Further, an HTGR produces U-233, which as seen in Table 4.1, is the most efficient fuel for thermal reactors. The HTGRs are also more efficient in heat losss, since 25 percent less heat is lost to the atmosphere by HTGRs than equivalent LWRs. This is possible because of specific constructional features associated with HTGRs and the higher temperatures produced in the steam or helium used for turbine power.

NOTES

1. Federal Power Commission, Hydroelectric Power Resources of the United States (Washington, D. C.: Government Printing Office, 1972), p. vii.

2. Federal Power Commission, The 1970 National Power Survey (Washington, D. C.: Government Printing Office, 1971), p. I-7-73.

3. Edison Electric Institute, Statistical Year Book of the Electric Utility Industry for 1973 (New York: Edison Electric Institute, 1974).

4. City of Seattle, Power Generation Alternatives (Seattle: Cone-Heiden Corporation, 1972).

CHAPTER

5

THE ECONOMICS OF ELECTRICITY SUPPLY

The supply of electrical energy is the result of investments in generation, transmission, and distribution facilities and the operation of these facilities. To an individual utility any decision to invest in and operate these facilities is related to the demand for electricity imposed at any time on the utility by the customers located in the region served by it. A proper assessment of demand by the utility is therefore essential to it in correctly planning its investment and construction schedules in the long run, and its maintenance, load sharing, and production schedules in the short run. The importance of long run demand forecasts for a supplier of electricity to make appropriate investments has increased in recent years owing to a lengthening of lead times in planning, design, and construction of economically viable generating plants. The heavy emphasis on suitable forecasting methodology in this book has been presented mainly in recognition of the vital importance of this area to the management of our electrical energy sector. The total information required for planning of total capacity and, in particular, the economic mix of different types of capacities to be invested in is much more complex than would be provided by a reliable forecast of energy demands only.

A distinctive feature in the demand for electricity is the nature of variations in the kilowatts of power demanded by customers at different times. If energy sales (kilowatt hours) were always in a constant ratio to load demanded (kilowatts), the provision of generating capacity would be a simple matter resting purely on forecasts of electrical energy demand extending over the planning horizon. However, in actual practice, periods of peak loads in kilowatts may be limited to brief intervals only, requiring the provision a large amount of generating capacity in kilowatts that is used only during short periods of excessive load demand. Considering a decompositon of total generating costs into a set of fixed costs that are related to plant size and capacity and a set of variable costs that depend on the amount of energy actually generated, the basis for an optimum plant mix becomes simple. That portion of the total kilowatt load that represents a stable demand will be planned for by provision of plants with low operating or variable costs, and the portion representing infrequent peaking demand will be provided for by plants with low fixed costs.

A THEORETICAL FRAMEWORK

Ralph Turvey[1] in his analysis of optimal pricing and investment in electricity supply, examines the economic rationale for minimum cost operation, given a certain plant mix on the one hand and deciding on the optimal plant mix given the characteristics of future demand on the other. Our concern is mainly with the planning of generating capacity in the long run; and hence elements of Turvey's analysis, which in varying forms have been presented in other works on the subject, have been kept in mind in developing the following approach.

It has been observed that plants with lower operating costs will be used for longer base loads and that those with higher operating costs will be used for shorter peaking periods. This means that a utility attempting to minimize costs of generation would have a system of priorities according to which plants with low variable (or marginal) costs would rank higher than those with larger marginal costs. In developing a valid theoretical approach, suppose that m_1 is the marginal cost of generating 1 KwH using a particular type of plant, and m_2 is the marginal cost of generating the same 1 KwH from another type of plant available at that instant. Then if $m_1 > m_2$, the plant with m_2 ranks higher than that with m_1; if $m_2 > m_1$, then the plant with m_1 ranks higher than m_2. Hence, for n different types of plants designated by i = 1, 2, 3, ... n in descending order of priority in operation, plant 1 will be operated for maximum output. Then for any given hour, the savings from operating a higher priority plant i that is available would be given by $(m_{i+1} - m_i)$.

If we knew the load perfectly for every hour of operation in the future, we could identify exactly which plant would be operating in a given hour and, consequently, the marginal cost of every unit of electricity generated. A new plant in which investment is being considered may be higher on the priority list of marginal cost, as in the case of nuclear plants, or lower as in the case of a gas-fired internal combustion turbine plant. Then the savings or loss, respectively, for each hour of operation by new plant in the future would be given by $(m_{i+1} - m_i)$ or $(m_{i-1} - m_i)$. In making a decision, the relevant measure for computation would be the present value of these savings or losses associated with each type of plant being considered; that is total savings or losses are given by

$$S_i = PV(m_{i+1} - m_i) x + PV(m_{i-1} - m_i) y$$

where $x + y = 1$ and $x = 1$ or 0; $y = 1$ or 0, and the expressions with PV indicate present values of the quantities within the brackets. Up to this point, only variable costs of generation have been considered; but there are in actual fact a set of fixed costs also that would enter the analysis. These consist of construction costs, interest payments, fixed maintenance costs, and so on and can be expressed in terms of an annuity A_i over the expected life of the plant of type i. Similarly, the savings function S_i can also be converted into an annuity S_i' for the same period. Then for every additional kilowatt of capacity installed in a plant of type i, the total increase in cost will be represented by an annuity of $(A_i - S_i')$. If n different types of plants are being considered, than the optimal plant mix will be given by the condition that $(A_i - S_i')$ for all i is the same. If this equality does not hold, a reallocation of total capacity between each type would result in decrease in total cost.

The theory presented above, undoubtedly, cannot be used in adopting a suitable plan for capacity augmentation, mainly because perfect knowledge of the future in such fine detail is not possible. The computation involved, though feasible by computer simulation, would be very expensive and cumbersome and, given the normal reliability of the data to be used, would involve a large cost without commensurate benefits. Besides, much greater complexity would have to be built into a simulation model to take into account factors such as maintenance schedules and breakdowns, all of which would again be of questionable value given the quality of information and data available as inputs to the model. The approach developed here, nevertheless, can be used broadly in determining present values or annuities related to different types of generating plants, given the future growth in demand for electrical energy in kilowatt hours and load in kilowatts. A unit period of a year can then be used in place of an hour, and given the peak load in kilowatts and the load factor for the system, the same analysis as presented above can provide useful information for decision making.

Such an approach has been used, in a very broad sense, to illustrate the economic differences in choice for the Carolina Power and Light system at the end of this chapter. At this stage, however, it is first necessary to examine specific costs related to different forms of power generation and some of the economic factors pertinent to each type. This study does not explore the nature or composition of transmission and distribution costs since they do not offer much

ECONOMICS OF ELECTRICITY SUPPLY

choice to the policy maker; and, therefore, construction and maintenance costs related to them generally can be assumed to be given without any serious loss of specificity in any economic comparison between supply alternatives.

The Federal Power Commission (FPC) publishes much data on the economics of generation. Unfortunately these valuable data, which have been selectively tabulated in this chapter, are not up to date due to a lag in collection and compilation by the commission. However, they do illustrate trends that may provide estimates for current and future values.

HYDROELECTRIC GENERATION

Since the characteristics of a hydroelectric plant depend to such an extent on the geographic features associated with its siting, costs usually vary vastly from plant to plant. As these geographic features cannot be duplicated from one plant to another, the investment actually made in a project depends on the type and scale of project selected, the cost of land acquired, and the costs of relocating such items as buildings, railroads, and highways. The per unit costs of buildings and generating equipment usually vary inversely with the pressure head of water used for driving the plant. For instance, according to the FPC's 1970 National Power Survey,[2] the estimated cost per unit of capacity (kilowatts) for powerhouse and equipment for a 100,000-Kw plant was $130 with a 100-foot head, but only $90 with a 400-foot head. That is the reason for the preference for single high dams over a series of low dams to exploit the total head available along a particular stretch of any river. Also, investment per unit is smaller for a larger turbine generator than a number of smaller units with the same aggregate capacity. Marginal or operating costs also vary inversely with pressure head and size of generating unit. Of the hydroelectric plants currently in operation, capital costs will generally be found to be in the range of $200 to $400 per kilowatt.

Data on costs of federally owned hydroelectric projects are not very useful since they are mainly multipurpose projects with irrigational and recreational facilities combined with power generation. Table 5.1 shows the capital costs of some hydroelectric plants either privately or publicly owned (other than by the federal government). Operating costs of hydroelectric plants are much lower than any other type, the difference usually being due to the extent of fuel costs incurred in other forms of generation.

TABLE 5.1

Capital Cost of Typical Conventional Hydroelectric Projects

					Cost of Plant (in thousands of dollars)						
Owner	Name of plant	Capacity (Mw)	Head (ft.)	In-Service Date	Land	Structures	Reservoirs, Dams, and such	Equipment	Roads and Trails	Total	Cost/KW	State
Privately Owned												
Central Maine Power Co.	Indian Pond	76.4	145	1954	738	2,608	7,175	4,739	371	15,631	208	Maine
New England Power Co.	Moore	140.4	150	1956	2,524	2,970	16,582	7,529	–	29,605	211	N.H.
Virginia Electric and Power Co.	Gaston	177.9	67	1963	7,724	1,797	24,195	9,957	53	43,726	246	N.C.
Same	Roanoke Rapids	100.1	75	1955	1,463	1,962	20,606	6,499	68	30,598	306	N.C.
Tapoco, Inc. (Aluminum Co. of America)	Chilhowee	50.0	57	1957	2,234	417	5,346	3,567	33	11,597	232	Tenn.
Alabama Power Co.	Bouldin	225.0	117	1967	6,084	5,502	18,986	8,448	11	39,031	173	Ala.
Same	Lay	177.0	81	1967	7,643	1,387	17,357	10,387	–	36,774	208	Ala.
Montana Power Co.	Cochrane	48.0	80	1958	59	983	5,379	3,904	82	10,407	217	Mont.
Idaho Power Co.	Hells Canyon	391.5	210	1967	1,131	2,278	51,507	10,893	–	65,809	168	Idaho
Same	Oxbow	190.0	115	1961	197	7,073	28,326	10,516	10	46,122	243	Idaho
Same	Brownlee	360.4	250	1958	11,671	6,059	39,148	11,638	–	68,517	190	Idaho
Pacific Power and Light Co.	Swift No. 1	204.0	350	1958	7,740	2,915	38,191	8,974	99	57,919	284	Wash.
Washington Water Power Co.	Cabnet Gorge	200.0	99	1952	7,375	7,548	16,195	12,524	823	44,465	222	Idaho
Same	Noxon Rapids	282.9	152	1959	31,101	6,887	28,119	18,472	88	84,667	299	Mont.
Portland General Electric Co.	Pelton	108.0	150	1957	233	2,731	11,855	5,165	648	20,632	191	Ore.
Same	Round Butte	247.1	315	1964	3,347	5,087	37,711	8,536	886	55,567	225	Ore.
Pacific Gas and Electric Co.	James B. Black	154.8	1,115	1965	3,660	1,779	50,324	5,009	1,084	61,856	309	Calif.
Southern California Edison Co.	Mammouth Pool	129.4	250	1960	161	1,626	17,857	6,388	520	26,552	205	Calif.
Public (non-federal)												
City of Seattle	Boundry	551.0	250	1967	582	13,480	48,758	28,027	486	91,333	166	Wash.
Grand River Dam Authority	Kerr	108.0	58	1964	11,539	3,750	9,627	7,197	216	32,329	299	Okla.
PUD No. 1 of Chelan County	Rocky Beach	711.6	92	1961	41,291	54,667	63,382	46,779	191	206,310	290	Wash.
PUD No. 1 of Douglas County	Wells	774.3	65	1967	30,540	25,639	36,560	27,814	263	120,816	156	Wash.
Grand County PUD	Priest Rapids	788.5	78	1961	2,413	8,549	76,560	46,409	–	133,931	170	Wash.
Same	Wanapum	831.3	80	1963	15,443	9,811	87,076	43,836	–	156,166	188	Wash.

Source: Federal Power Commission, The 1970 National Power Survey (Washington, D. C.: Government Printing Office, 1971), p. IV-1-74.

ECONOMICS OF ELECTRICITY SUPPLY

TABLE 5.2

Conventional Steam-Electric Plant Data
for Selected Years from 1938-72

Year	1938	1947	1957	1967	1970	1971	1972
Number of plants	1,165	1,045	1,039	971	981	985	979
Installed capacity in megawatts	26,066	36,035	99,500	210,237	258,768	275,583	294,049
Average plant size in megawatts	22	35	96	217	264	280	300
Net generation in billion kilowatt hours	68.4	174.5	497.2	974.1	1242.3	1282.2	1378.3
Average annual plant factor	35	55	57	53	55	53	54

Source: Federal Power Commission, Steam-Electric Plant Construction Cost and Annual Production Expenses (Washington, D.C.: Government Printing Office, 1972).

CONVENTIONAL STEAM-ELECTRIC GENERATION

The per unit costs of electricity generated by conventional steam-electric plants has been steadily on the decline in recent years. This seems to be mainly the result of increases in size of generating units and of plants. The average unit size of generating stations increased from 700 Mw to 1300 Mw in 1972. The growth of plant sizes in the United States can be seen from 1938-72 in Table 5.2.

It can be observed from this table that, although the total number of plants in this period has declined steadily, a substantial increase in plant size resulted in almost a tenfold increase in the actual total capacity available.

Another important feature that has resulted in significant economies in generation is the reduction in unit heat rates. This development, as mentioned in the previous chapter, has slowed down considerably in the 1970s since technical improvements resulting in the use of superheated steam at high temperatures and pressures have reached a plateau.

Technical developments and unit sizes are, however, intimately related; and an increase in plant and generating unit sizes has been made possible by all-around progress in steel forging technology and in design and manufacture of handling equipment, bearings, and so on. Increases in size have been sought by electric utilities because of the accompanying reduction in capital costs with increasing unit size. Figure 5.1 shows the reduction in capital costs with increasing unit size.

Although improvements in the technical sphere are expected to continue with associated economic benefits up to 1990 and beyond, the change is not likely to be as dramatic as that witnessed in past decades. One reason for this lies in the fact that supercritical temperatures and pressures of steam used in generation probably will not increase substantially in the future. The economics of further temperature and pressure increases are not favorable, even though technically feasible. The increased capital costs required for thicker boiler walls, piping, and some auxiliary equipment are not likely to be offset fully by a reduction in fuel and other operating costs. This outlook could conveivably change with unforseen improvements in design and metallurgy, or high fuel costs.

A serious limitation with steam-electric units is the long hours that are necessary to start combustion in the boiler heating unit before steam is generated at a sufficiently high rate for running the generator units. This feature, as well as the lower operating costs of steam plants as against internal combustion turbines, has made at least the newer steam units more suitable for base-load operation. However, in the next few decades the large proportion of nuclear plants in operation at substantially lower variable costs would relegate today's conventional plants to peak load service only. This may require daily start-ups of boilers to meet daily peaks in demand and in effect would increase the fixed costs of such plants, since for a large proportion of the day they would be burning fuel merely in preparation for a possible few hours of actual generation. The problem of peak loads, therefore, is likely to impose much heavier costs on the system in the future than is the case today. This may lead to retirement of some conventional steam plants for replacement by internal combustion turbine plants, which have low capital costs and relatively short time of construction. Individual utilities should consider seriously the sale of some of their conventional steam plants in the next few years both as a solution to (1) the short run prospect of excess capacity in the industry and (2) the long run possibility of being saddled with conventional steam capacity useful only for peak load operation at significantly higher costs than other alternatives. It may be possible to export whole plants to countries embarking on rapid electrification schemes, particularly in the Middle East. At any rate, a reversal of the trend in rapid build-up of conventional steam plant capacity is taking place and is likely to continue in the

FIGURE 5.1

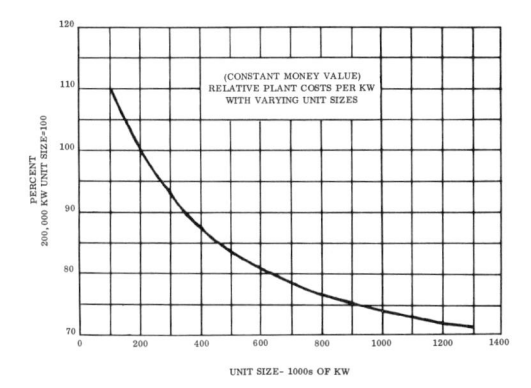

Relationship Between Plant Costs and Unit Sizes

Source: Federal Power Commission, The 1970 National Power Survey (Washington, D. C.: Government Printing Office, 1971), part 4, pp. 1-6.

TABLE 5.3

Investments in Conventional Steam-Powered Generation in the United States

Year	Capacity Installed (megawatts)	Plant Investment (thousands of dollars)	Cost (dollars per kilowatt)
1967	4,165	452,422	109
1968	5,115	626,885	123
1969	2,483	310,008	125
1970	4,863	793,287	163
1971	9,067	1,239,448	137
1972	5,347	800,486	150

Source: Federal Power Commission, Steam-Electric Plant Construction Cost and Annual Production Expenses (Washington, D. C.: Government Printing Office, 1974).

future as opposed to the trend seen in Table 5.3, which displays the increase in capacity in recent years, even with steadily rising capital costs. A comparison between these costs and those shown in Table 5.1 indicates that capital costs associated with conventional steam generation are substantially lower than with hydroelectric projects.

In investigating the economics of electric plant operation, the single most important cost item is per unit cost of fuel used in generation. Although the basic technology of power generation in conventional steam plants is similar for the different types of fuel in use, there are significant constructional differences requiring a decision on the fuel type to be used when a plant is in its design phase. Of course, plants often have been converted from one fuel use to the other, incurring relatively modest expenditures to implement such conversions; but most utilities avoid such action since it often causes problems in transportation, handling, and storage of fuel and disposal of residues, which are costly in terms of managerial attention and time.

In arriving at a particular fuel choice for generation, apart from the expected market selling price for fuel itself, it is important to consider several types of costs.

(1) Transportation. Often this component can be a significant proportion of total fuel costs, particularly in the case of coal, which involves heavy tonnages in movement. For this reason, coal-based plants are often located close to mines.

(2) Handling. Costs of handling again are usually in direct proportion to the bulk of fuel used, and this factor works unfavorably against coal. To this also must be added the running costs of ash removal and handling that are incurred in coal-burning plants.

(3) Conversion efficiency. Fuels are available in various grades of thermal content and the relevant fuel costs measure to be considered in any choice is the cost per kilowatt hour of electricity generated.

(4) Pollution control. It is difficult to estimate the effects of future regulation in this area; but even on the basis of existing air pollution regulations, the costs associated with compliance can be estimated with reasonable accuracy. The Environmental Protection Agency (EPA) in its Survey of Processes and Costs for SO_2 Control on Steam-Electric Power Plants (1971) computed costs of SO_2 removal by different processes. Assuming a 55 percent load factor, 3.5 percent sulfur content in coal with a thermal content of 11,800 Btu/lb, an example of estimated costs for two of the eight processes is given below for a 100-Mw plant.

Capital cost	($/Kw)	$11.6 and $36.0
Operating cost	(mills/KwH)	0.82 and 0.39

Sulfur dioxide removal costs contribute substantially not only to operating costs but also the capital cost of a plant as well. These costs can be avoided or at least decreased with the use of low sulfur coal, but supplies of that in the eastern United States are concentrated in Appalachia

ECONOMICS OF ELECTRICITY SUPPLY

and occur in limited quantities. Most of the low sulfur coal reserves in the United States exist in the western states, and for these to be used by eastern concerns such as Carolina Power and Light would increase transport costs substantially.

As a result of the costs associated with the use of coal as a fuel, many utilities preferred investments in oil-burning plants and, in some cases, converted existing coal based plants to oil before the increase in oil prices in 1973-74. The pollution problem with oil generally is not as costly as with coal. Residual fuel oil usually has a high sulfur content but can be used by blending with low sulfur oil from Africa to meet existing sulfur emission control regulations. The oil industry currently is making heavy investments in the construction of new hydrodesulfurization and blending facilities; and this development, along with a stabilization of oil prices, may again lead to a greater effort toward conversion of coal based plants to residual oil. The change in proportions between the three primary fuels used in power generation in the United States can be seen in Table 5.4.

Of the three, the greatest decline in use is likely to take place in the use of natural gas in steam-powered generation, as the result of a deliberate policy being followed by the FPC and the Federal Energy Administration (FEA) to ease the gas shortages that are developing rapidly. Natural gas has been a very popular fuel for steam-powered plants due to its nonpolluting properites and substantially lower costs per British thermal unit. The differentials in costs paid by electric utilities in using these three fuels for steam-electric generation are brought out in Table 5.5.

In addition to fuel expenses, other costs of generation include maintenance costs and wages of personnel associated with the generating plant. Large coal-fired units require relatively more maintenance and are usually scheduled for four to six weeks of outage annually. Gas-fired boilers require the least time for maintenance. Personnel and other costs usually display economies of scale, with costs per kilowatt decreasing with larger capacity generating plants.

The breakdown of total generating costs for steam-powered plants in the United States is given in Table 5.6 for the years 1958-72.

GAS TURBINE GENERATION

The gas turbine units currently available in the market are usually up to 60,000 Kw in capacity. As mentioned earlier, their low capital costs and short lead time in construction make them a good choice for peaking operation. A normal generating plant with 10 to 15 individual turbine units can be easily constructed and brought under operation

TABLE 5.4

Percentages of Different Fossil Fuels Used in
Steam-Powered Generation in the United States

Year	Coal	Gas	Oil
1967	64	27	9
1968	61	29	10
1969	60	28	12
1970	57	29	14
1971	55	29	16
1972	54	26	20

Source: Federal Power Commission, Steam-Electric Plant Construction Cost and Annual Production Expenses (Washington, D.C.: Government Printing Office, 1974), p. xvii.

TABLE 5.5

Cost of Fossil-Fuels Burned for
Steam-Powered Generation in the United States
in cents/million Btu

Year	Coal	Gas	Oil	Weighted average
1962	25.6	26.4	34.5	26.5
1963	25.0	25.5	33.5	25.8
1964	24.5	25.4	32.7	25.3
1965	24.4	25.0	33.1	25.2
1966	24.7	25.0	32.4	25.4
1967	25.2	24.7	32.2	25.7
1968	25.5	25.1	32.8	26.1
1969	26.6	25.4	31.9	26.9
1970	31.1	27.0	36.6	30.7
1971	36.0	28.0	51.5	26.4
1972	38.1	20.3	58.8	39.9
1973	41.9	35.2	78.3	48.4

Source: Federal Power Commission, Steam-Electric Plant Construction Cost and Annual Production Expenses (Washington, D.C.: Government Printing Office, 1974), p. xvii; and Edison Electric Institute, Statistical Year Book of the Electric Utility Industry for 1973 (New York: Edison Electric Institute, 1974), p. 50.

TABLE 5.6

Annual Generating Costs for Conventional
Steam-Powered Plants in the United States
mills per kilowatt hour

Year	Operation	Maintenance	Subtotal	Fuel	Total
1958	0.51	0.40	0.91	2.94	3.85
1959	0.47	0.38	0.85	2.82	3.67
1960	0.47	0.38	0.85	2.81	3.66
1961	0.44	0.37	0.81	2.78	3.59
1962	0.42	0.37	0.79	2.75	3.54
1963	0.40	0.35	0.75	2.66	3.41
1964	0.38	0.36	0.74	2.64	3.38
1965	0.38	0.37	0.75	2.60	3.35
1966	0.37	0.36	0.73	2.61	3.34
1967	0.38	0.39	0.77	2.65	3.42
1968	0.37	0.38	0.75	2.68	3.43
1969	0.37	0.39	0.76	2.77	3.53
1970	0.38	0.45	0.83	3.15	3.98
1971	0.42	0.52	0.94	3.77	4.71
1972	0.42	0.57	0.99	4.06	5.05

Source: Federal Power Commission, Steam-Electric Plant Construction Cost and Annual Production Expenses (Washington, D.C.: Government Printing Office, 1974), p. xxviii.

well within two years. Capital costs range between $75 to $100/Kw for the entire plant, which compares favorably with conventional steam plants having at least 50 percent higher capital costs. Thermal efficiencies of these plants, are, however, much lower and usually average 14,000 Btu per KwH. At 1972 average prices, this would give a fuel cost per kilowatt hour of 4.242 mills which, in spite of the lower costs per British thermal unit of gas, works out higher than the weighted average fuel cost per kilowatt hour for 1972 given in Table 5.6. In actual fact, since gas turbines use higher grade fuels only, the cost per kilowatt hour in 1972 was usually well above 5.0 mills. As such, these plants are operated in periods of peak demand only, and the low capital costs, when distributed over the relatively low energy output, consequently increase the total cost per kilowatt hour, which in 1972 was often in the range of 12 to 15 mills. Rough estimates of these costs at present are in the region of 15 to 20 mills/KwH; and with the prospect of shortages of natural gas in the future, these may increase at the rate of up to 10 percent a year in the future unless technical changes in design of gas turbine plants can bring about improvements in thermal efficiencies.

NUCLEAR GENERATION

Nuclear generation is still in its infancy and rapid changes will continue to take place in design, construction, maintenance, and operation of nuclear plants. The experience thus far has been marked with high outages of plants, and it is difficult to predict maintenance costs with any accuracy, particularly because nuclear plants have not been in operation long enough. However, it is reasonable to expect that with increasing expertise in maintenance, inherently lower steam conditions in nuclear as opposed to fossil-fuel plants, and the absence of conventional steam boilers, forced outages and maintenance costs in nuclear plants will be relatively lower than in conventional steam plants.

TABLE 5.7

New Capacity Additions Announced in the
United States for 300 Megawatts and Above

Year	Percent of Total Nuclear	Fossil	Capacity (in megawatts) Nuclear	Fossil
1970	31	69	13,491	29,910
1971	52	48	31,810	29,372
1972	49	51	42,473	44,281
1973*	57	43	31,706	24,119

*First nine months.
Source: Federal Power Commission, Steam-Electric Plant Construction Cost and Annual Production Expenses (Washington, D. C.: Government Printing Office, 1974), p. xiv.

The trend toward an increasing share for nuclear power in the nation's future generating potential is brought out by Table 5.7 showing the new capacity additions announced in the United States for the years 1970-73 published by the FPC. The average capital cost of nuclear units has been increasing steadily. In the period 1965-68, the average capital cost of new units ordered was approximately $150/Kwe (kilowatts of nuclear generating potential). In 1972, according to the FPC the average capital cost of units in operation was $178/Kwe. The cost of units ordered in 1972 was, however, estimated at about $429/Kwe and for 1973 at $449/Kwe. These estimates do not account for delays in construction and commissioning, which would increase capital costs considerably due to larger wage bills and interest charges during construction. The 1970 National Power Survey had predicted a decrease in capital costs to the extent of about $10-15/Kwe on account of expected cost reductions brought about by increased business volume and greater experience in construction techniques and component design. However, this decrease has not been realized. In fact, estimates by electric utility executives indicate capital costs in the region of $500/Kwe and over.

Delays are of vital concern to utilities investing in nuclear power. Scheduled commercial operation is being put back in most projects by two to four years due to late deliveries of equipment, mistakes in installation, strikes and go-slow actions, bad weather during construction, detailed Atomic Energy Commission (AEC) reviews, and opposition by environmentalists and other citizens' groups. These factors combined with the financial problems facing electric utilities (described in the following chapters) could very well increase capital costs of nuclear plants by about 8-10 percent a year in the next decade.

Fuel costs for nuclear generation consist of a number of distinct components. Costs of each were analyzed in the 1970 National Power Survey, but updated data for the present are not yet available. A recent study by Seymour Baron[3] forecasts costs of nuclear fuel for light water reactors (LWR) as follows (in terms of constant 1974 dollars):

Year	Enriched Uranium (mills/KwH)	Reasons for Increase
1977	1.6	—
1985	1.8	Due to waste storage
2000	2.0	Yellow cake* > $8.00/lb
2020	2.5	Yellow cake > $15.00/lb

*Yellow cake is the commercial name for uranium oxide.

Fuel materials The AEC is confident that reserves in this country are adequate to supply fuel needs for the foreseeable future. However, the supply curve for uranium, as for any other commodity, is upward sloping, and additional quantities can be located and mined only at increasing marginal costs. As of January 1, 1970, the estimated exploitable resources of uranium stood as indicated in Table 5.8. There is, however, considerable debate on the AEC's optimism; and even though known reserves in other countries such as Canada and South Africa are abundant, a serious further effort is in the offing

TABLE 5.8

Estimates of Exploitable Resources of Uranium

	Uranium Deposits	By-product
Less than $10		
Reasonably Assured Resources	250,000	90,000
Estimated Additional Resources	600,000	—
$10 to $15		
Reasonably Assured Resources	140,000	20,000
Estimated Additional Resources	300,000	—

Source: Federal Power Commission, The 1970 National Power Survey (Washington, D. C.: Goverment Printing Office, 1971), p. V-1-50.

to discover additional supplies within the United States. This may result in higher prices than anticipated.

Conversion to UF_6 (uranium hexaflouride or fluoride of uranium) Uranium ore must be refined to U_3O_8 (oxide of uranium) and UF_6 for enrichment. The base price for this process in 1970 was $1.04/lb for uranium and is likely to gradually go down to $0.92/lb for uranium in 1985 and hold steady at that level thereafter.

Enrichment Enrichment of U-235 is controlled by the government, and the cost of this since September 1971 has been $32.00/Kg (kilogram). Enrichment costs are not likely to increase substantially in the future.

Fabrication Fabrication of fuel to be inserted into the reactor in appropriate form is currently expensive. From a cost of about $80/Kg in 1970, economies of scale are likely to reduce this figure to about $60 in 1980 and $45 in 1990. Beyond that year, however, costs are likely to rise again due to complexities expected in fabrication and handling of fuels for advanced types of reactors.

Reprocessing Spent fuel exhausted from the reactor is reprocessed to extract usable nuclear fuel. These costs are also likely to follow the pattern of fabrication costs and may decrease to $27/Kg in 1980 and $20/Kg in 1990 from the 1970 cost of $31/Kg. But again, increases are expected beyond 1990 for the same reasons.

Shipping costs The FPC's estimate of shipping costs indicate that the cost of shipping new fuel after fabrication to the generation site is about one-sixth the cost of shipping spent fuel from the plant for reprocessing. These costs in 1970 were around $4.00/Kg and by the mid-1970s were in the neighborhood of $6.00/Kg. Future costs are likely to rise at approximately 10 percent a year.

Financing costs These costs enter into fuel costs on account of the need for working capital tied up in all the elements of the fuel cycle described above. John N. Vernon[4] estimated working capital cost as being 18 percent of total fuel costs. This is much higher than working capital costs for a conventional steam plant, and the precise figure naturally will vary with prevailing interest rates. From Vernon's figures, the author has computed the variation of working capital costs expressed as a percentage of total fuel costs against different prevailing interest rates.

Percentage interest rate	6	8	10	12	16	20	24
Working capital as percentage of fuel costs	12	15.7	18.0	20.8	25.8	29.6	33.9

Total fuel costs, including all the elements described above, were estimated by the FPC; and in the 1970 National Power Survey these were projected into the future. The FPC forecasts of fuel costs were considerably lower than Baron's mentioned earlier. Any forecasting exercise in this area has to take into account a large number of uncertainties; and perhaps Baron's estimates, on the basis of present indicators, appear more realistic.

Having discussed and investigated the nature and magnitude of various generating costs, in the following section an attempt is made to show how the choice of a specific set of generation alternatives can influence costs of generating electric power to meet future demand.

AN ILLUSTRATIVE EXAMPLE IN CAPACITY PLANNING

Earlier in this chapter a theoretical framework was developed for deciding on what type of plant to build and use for each additional kilowatt of load that would be imposed on the supplier in the future. The rationale for this decision was found to be a comparison of present values of costs of different generation alternatives for every hour of operation. In practice, however, a strict application of this approach is not possible, because one would require precise information not only on the actual kilowatt demand for each future hour but also on the availability of each type of plant during each hour. Nevertheless, one could treat a year as the time unit for planning and the load demanded can be expressed in terms of three measures: (1) total annual kilowatt hours of energy demanded, (2) the load factor expected to be achieved for the utility's system, and (3) the maximum peak demand during the year. The latter two variables among these can be regarded as proxies for the actual hour-to-hour fluctuations in the energy demanded during the year. Alternative generating plans can then be tested for merit by a comparison of present values of the costs involved in adopting each of these plans to meet projected demand.

To illustrate this approach, alternative plans for augmenting kilowatt capacity for the Carolina Power and Light system to meet forecasted demand for the period mid-1975 to mid 1990 will be evaluated. The starting point for this exercise is, therefore, a dynamic forecast of demand for this time span, which has already been developed in Part I of this book. The steps to be followed in evaluating the economic merits of alternative plans can be summarized as explained below.

(1) <u>Forecasting of annual demand in kilowatt hours</u>: this is provided by the output from the dynamic forecasting model in Part I. The forecasts used are based on a two-month increase in prices of 0.9 percent for electricity, fuel oil for heating, and coal and natural gas for residential and business consumption. The model was modified to provide aggregate demand for the Carolina Power and Light system on an annual basis commencing July 1975. The annual time periods for which demand was forecasted are therefore 1975-76, 1976-77, and so on until 1989-90, and this is shown against million kilowatt hours demanded in Table 5.9.

(2) <u>Determination of kilowatt capacity required</u>: the two assumptions used in determining the kilowatt generating capacity required by the utility are (a) the average load factor for the system continues to be 60 percent, which is approximately what Carolina Power and Light has been able to achieve in the 1970s (59.9 percent in 1973 and 61.3 percent in 1972) and is also close enough to the national average, which was 62.0 percent in 1973 but somewhat higher in previous years; (b) the percentage reserve capacity available in the system to meet peaks in demand is desired to be kept constant over the planning period. The desired reserve capacity in the Carolina Power and Light system has been assumed to be 13 percent over the average annual load. (It was actually 13.3 percent in the peak load month of August 1974). It is possible that, through greater coordination with other utilities and some additional pricing measures to be described

ECONOMICS OF ELECTRICITY SUPPLY 115

TABLE 5.9

Kilowatt Capacity Required for Meeting Future Demand

Year	Total Energy Demand (in million KwH)	Average Load (in thousand Kw)	Required Capacity (average load and 13 percent reserve)
1975-76	24139.5	4592.75	5189.8
1976-77	24623.6	4684.85	5293.9
1977-78	25703.6	4890.33	5526.1
1978-79	26633.3	5067.16	5725.9
1979-80	27439.2	5220.55	5899.2
1980-81	28277.1	5379.95	6079.34
1981-82	29220.1	5559.38	6282.1
1982-83	30104.6	5727.67	6472.3
1983-84	31112.7	5919.46	6689.0
1984-85	32142.1	6115.30	6910.3
1985-86	33292.6	6334.21	7157.6
1986-87	35540.1	6571.53	7425.8
1987-88	35910.0	6832.19	7720.4
1988-89	37439.5	7123.19	8049.2
1989-90	39195.1	7457.21	8426.6

Source: Compiled by author.

later, the individual reserve requirements for the utility's own generating capacity can be reduced. However, for this illustrative exercise, the conservative estimate of 13 percent will be retained for the entire planning period. The two assumptions made here indicate that the pattern of load demand fluctuations is not expected to change appreciably, and further limitations such as plant outages and availability will continue to restrict the achievement of the system load factor to only 60 percent. The energy demand forecasts together with the 60 percent load and 13 percent reserve assumptions enable one to calculate desired kilowatt capacity for each year. This is given by

$$\text{Kw capacity} = \frac{\text{KwH}}{\text{load factor} \times 8760} \times 1.13$$

The values computed for each year are shown in Table 5.9 in thousand kilowatts.

(3) Determination of plant sizes: the adoption of particular plant sizes for capacity additions depends to a large extent, on the utility's perception of growth in demand. If there were no economies of scale

reflected both in capital and operating costs, theoretically a utility would like to add to its generating potential in small steps of kilowattage exactly equal to the increase in load (including a suitable reserve) expected for each time period. However, economies of scale weigh heavily in favor of installing plants larger than immediately desired, even though a high proportion of the new capacity goes unutilized in the first few years. The expectation that justifies this approach in economic terms is that if demand is increasing rapidly, the delay in full utilization of capacity will be brief, and consequently the loss due to higher capital costs will be such as to be offset by economies of scale in using one large plant as against setting up small plants at frequent time intervals. On the other hand, if demand growth is slow, construction of large generating plants will result in long initial periods of unutilized capacity and unjustified fixed costs. In such a situation the utility may install lower sized units at shorter intervals with scale diseconomies rather than large ones spaced over long periods of time.

It is expected, however, that the prospect of lower growth in demand will not bring about a reversal in the trend toward larger sizes, mainly because (a) most utilities are now moving toward better coordination in power sharing, thus reducing the possibility of large unutilized generating capacity, and (b) economies of scale in both conventional steam plants and nuclear units are considerable. In this planning exercise, a unit size of 1,050 Mw for nuclear plants and 720 Mw for fossil-fuel based steam plants has been adopted. These are in keeping with Carolina Power and Light's current plans for expansion, and it has been assumed that these sizes have been adopted by the utility on the basis of such factors as transportation costs, availability of construction facilities, and design know-how.

(4) <u>Specification of actual alternative plans</u>: using the information outlined thus far, specific plans for the construction and installation of additional capacity can now be set. The utility planner, in trying to choose the optimal plant mix, would evolve a number of alternative choices, each of which will be subjected to economic evaluation. In this exercise, three options have been adopted: (a) the all-nuclear option, (b) the all-fossil-fuel based conventional steam option, and (c) the internal combustion turbine generator (ICTG) capacity balancing option, which is in effect a variation of the second option.

The Carolina Power and Light performance figures for 1973 indicate that for the four different types of generating plants in use, plant factors for each group as a distinct unit were as follows: fossil-fuel based steam plants—59.3 percent, nuclear plants—62.8 percent, ICTG plants—13.1 percent, hydroelectric plants—47.6 percent. For the reasons described earlier, the ICTGs were used largely for peaking periods, and to an appreciable extent so were the hydroelectric units. In this planning exercise, it has been assumed that these individual percentages in load factors will not change in the future except in the case of option (c), which uses a greater extent of ICTG generation. Again, this is predicated on the supposition that fluctuations in load, limitations imposed by outages, maintenance procedures in each type of plant, and refueling in the case of nuclear plants will restrict load factors for each group to these figures.

With commissioning of the Brunswick no. 2 plant in 1975, the Carolina Power and Light system capacity at the start of the 1975-76 year can be taken to be 6,815 thousand Kw. However, the similarity of the model with Carolina Power and Light's actual expansion plan stops here. For purposes of illustrating planning methodology, at this stage no cognizance has been taken of any ongoing construction activity within the system or any financial commitments that may result in plant additions in the period 1975-90. The additions proposed in this example will be purely the result of the analysis being presented, and to that extent may be considered as hypothetical.

The plant additions proposed are arrived at by comparing the total kilowatt hour energy demand for the year with the sum of kilowatt hours actually produced by each group of plants, so the respective load factors are not exceeded. In sharing the total kilowatt hour demand, it has been calculated that the ICTG plants will have to generate a minimum of 640.2 million KwH and the hydroelectric plant a minimum of 894.83 million KwH to meet peaking demands. These outputs are the same values as those generated in 1973. The balance of the energy demanded will be shared by first generating as much as possible by nuclear generation and the remainder by fossil-fuel steam plants, ensuring at all times that the load factors for each group are not exceeded. The preference for nuclear generation using the given capacities in each year is dictated by lower marginal costs.

The plan for capacity additions using this approach is clearcut in respect to options (a) and (b) and yields the following plans:

option (a)—construction of 1050-Mw nuclear plants only (first plant for operation by mid-1983; second plant for operation by mid-1987);
option (b)—construction of 720-Mw conventional steam plants only (first plant for operation by mid-1983, second plant for operation by mid-1986, and third plant for operation by mid-1988).

In option (c) it has been decided that the first conventional steam plant, due for operation in 1983 as above, will not be constructed. Instead, it has been assumed that the company will use its existing ICTG plants to take up the slack for the period up to mid-1987, when a new conventional steam plant is brought into operation. During the period 1983-87 this option requires the use of ICTG plants with a plant factor of 48.6

percent, which is achieved in the year 1986-87. Beyond that year, the ICTGs are relegated again to peaking service, functioning with a load factor of 13.1 percent. The additional demand is then taken up by setting up another conventional steam plant and bringing it into operation by mid-1988. The purpose in taking option (c) into consideration is to see how a plan that uses an alternative with higher operating costs but economizes on capital costs compares with the other two options described.

Option (c) requires the following conventional steam plant additions to capacity: first plant for operation by mid-1987 and second plant for operation by mid-1988.

(5) <u>Computation of present values of the alternative plans</u>: in computation of present values, which provide the final economic evaluation of these plans, several cost assumptions are made in accordance with the discussion on costs presented earlier: total capital costs spread over the construction life of a plant are conventional steam, $150/Kw; nuclear, $500/Kw. Since these costs are the cumulative capital expenditures made over the construction phase of each type of plant, it is necessary to determine the timing of cash flows constituting the total capital costs assumed above. For this purpose, data were obtained from the North Carolina Utilities Commission to determine the broad subdivisions within which capital expenditures have been taking place. The break-down for a typical nuclear plant was found to be

Category	Percent
Land and land rights	1.9
Structures and improvements	22.0
Reactor plant equipment	31.0
Turbine plant equipment	12.8
Accessory electrical equipment	5.0
General plant equipment	0.7
Switchyard	1.8
Interest during construction	16.2
Nuclear fuel and start-up	8.6
Total	100.0

The timing of these expenditures varied considerably from plant to plant, but for each year of construction an average was computed in percentage terms and is represented by the following cash flow diagram reduced to $500/Kw.

ECONOMICS OF ELECTRICITY SUPPLY

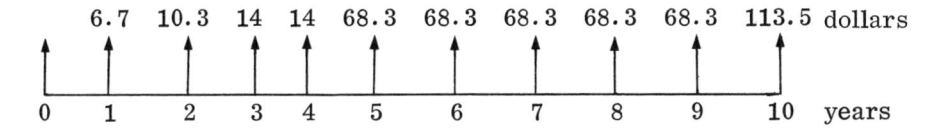

```
  6.7  10.3   14   14  68.3  68.3  68.3  68.3  68.3  113.5 dollars
   ↑    ↑     ↑    ↑    ↑     ↑     ↑     ↑     ↑     ↑
┌──┴────┴─────┴────┴────┴─────┴─────┴─────┴─────┴─────┴──────
0   1    2    3    4    5     6     7     8     9    10   years
```

The total period of construction of 10 years adopted here is based on 1975 estimates, but slippages of two to four years could easily occur in the future on account of some of the reasons mentioned earlier. However, this time schedule is in keeping with the planning schedule for an LWR plant adopted by the Policy Study Group of the Massachusetts Institute of Technology Energy Laboratory in the article "Energy Self-Sufficiency: An Economic Evaluation."[5]

On the other hand, the time span for a fossil-fuel based steam generating plant during construction was found to be approximately half that of an LWR nuclear plant. In a similar fashion, the typical cash flows in construction of a fossil-fuel plant for a total capital cost of $150/Kw were found to be as in the following diagram:

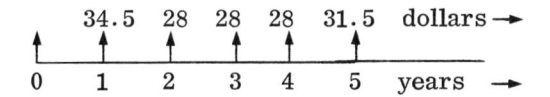

```
  34.5   28   28   28   31.5  dollars →
   ↑     ↑    ↑    ↑     ↑
┌──┴─────┴────┴────┴─────┴──────────
0   1    2    3    4     5    years →
```

Since conventional steam and nuclear plants are the only two types of plants considered for construction in the three options evaluated, assumptions on capital costs of ICTG or hydroelectric plants were not required. The operating or marginal costs of each type of generation for 1975-76 have been assumed to be as follows: fossil-fuel based steam generation, 5.85 mills/KwH; nuclear, 2.90 mills/KwH; hydroelectric, 1.16 mills/KwH; and ICTG, 8.68 mills/KwH. These values are in accordance with the cost estimates and discussion presented earlier in this chapter.

These marginal costs have been assumed to escalate at annual rates of 5 percent for conventional steam and nuclear plants and 8 percent for ICTG plants, respectively, in real terms. Hydroelectric marginal costs have been assumed to remain constant for the entire planning period. These assumptions have been predicated mainly on the future outlook for fuel costs. Whereas a true picture of fossil and nuclear fuel costs in the future is somewhat hazy, it seems certain that the cost of natural gas for power generation will continue to rise sharply through the simulated period 1975-90. Both the FEA and the FPC are pursuing a set of policies limiting the use of natural gas for power generation, and the future demands of electric utilities are likely to be met with gas to be allocated for this purpose only at higher prices and in lower quantities. Should controls on the price of natural gas be reduced or eliminated by some measure of deregulation price increases may for some periods be sharper than the assumption of a steady 8 percent annual increase. At any rate, the long run rate of annual increase, even with complete deregulation, may not be higher than a real increase of 8 percent, as some studies in this area would suggest.

The discount rate used for computation of present values in this exercise is 8 percent, which has been adopted in view of the fact that the North Carolina Utilities Commission attempts to set electric rates so the utility concerned is able to earn a fair rate of return of 8 percent after taxes. Using these assumptions, the present values of costs associated with generation of electrical energy over the period 1975-90 were found to be

option (a)–all-nuclear construction, $2,225,543 \times 10^3$;
option (b)–all-conventional steam plant construction, $1,914,592 \times 10^3$; and
option (c)–limited conventional steam plant construction, $1,866,873 \times 10^3$.

These figures indicate that the cost of generating electrical energy under these conditions is very sensitive to capital costs. Option (c), which involves the use of ICTG generation to a large degree, is the least expensive of the three in spite of much higher marginal costs. Option (a), on the other hand, is significantly higher in spite of much lower marginal cost per kilowatt hour. To test how option (a) would respond to a more intensive use of nuclear capacity, it was assumed that the nuclear plants in this case could be run at higher efficiency represented by a load factor of 85 percent. When the present value of costs for option (a) using this assumption was computed, it yielded a figure of $2,089,876.

Although this example may suggest that the path that the utility should follow is that of making more intensive use of its ICTG capacity, making minimum additions to its conventional steam generating potential, and completely abandoning nuclear plant additions, this author advocates the opposite. There are definite social benefits and political merits in pursuing a build-up in nuclear power capacity–a moment's reflection on the events of 1973-75 provides adequate proof. A deep dependence on fossil-fuels for power generation implies an insecure reliance on the OPEC (Organization of Petroleum Exporting Countries cartel and a half dozen countries in the Middle East, which this nation cannot possibly accept on political grounds.

However, the point proved by the present value computations is that the cost per kilowatt hour of electricity generated in the future will depend to a great extent on the construction programs and expansion of capacity pursued by a utility. Hence, capacity expansion should be restricted to the barest minimum. This, no doubt, is easier said than done. Being used to the growth rates in energy demand of the last decade and naturally concerned about the possibility of severe brownouts and blackouts in the future, few utility executives are likely to make drastic changes in their construction plans. But unless this is done now, their problems will be compounded by price-induced cutbacks in quantity demanded by customers, consequent growth in surplus generating capacity, and increases in the cost of borrowing money for construction, all of which would further increase the price of electricity—the cycle would thus continue.

In these computations, a fixed decision function has been assumed for capacity expansion, which in effect depends on the variables representing the expected quantity of energy demanded, a given fixed peaking reserve, and a time span up to 1990 for present value calculations. The results would be in favor of nuclear generation with a longer time consideration, as is usually the case. In actual practice the capacity decision would be a function of the expected value of quantity demanded and the variance associated with this value, in the predictions available. In other words, capacity planning may not depend on a fixed percentage reserve, but rather on the variability associated with a particular set of energy forecasts. There may be, therefore, some rational basis for the plans for large capacity expansion that most utilities still retain in spite of falling rages of growth in demand. Energy forecasts no longer inspire the confidence of utility planners, and this fact is perhaps reflected in the provision of large capacity reserves for future generation. A significant cutback in expansion plans, therefore, can be brought about by the development of rigorous and robust forecasting methodologies and sensitivity analyses of predicted outcomes in response to varied assumptions in economic phenomena.

THE ECONOMIC BENEFITS OF COORDINATION

An important feature in the supply of electricity, which could result in significant reductions in the provision of individual reserves by a particular utility, is the coordination of power generation between it and other utilities. The problem of coordination has drawn a good deal of attention in recent years. The 1964 National Power Survey carried out a study of the extent and economic effects of coordination perceived during that year. The 1970 survey gave this subject even greater attention and coverage. The history of intersystem coordination in the United States actually extends as far back as the 1920s, when a few utilities had standing arrangements for sale and purchase of excess electricity with neighboring utilities. The practice has grown steadily in the past decades and most electric utilities now have some degree of of formal coordination with neighboring systems. This is indicated by the FPC figures, which show that from nine power pools with 23 percent of U.S. generating potential in 1960, the extent of coordination had grown to form 22 pools with 60 percent of total capacity in 1970.

Coordination can be achieved by different degrees of joint planning and operation. From an informal arrangement to buy and sell power when possible, on the one hand, two coordinating utilities could extend the concept to a close relationship in planning facilities on the other. Coordinated planning could include joint decisions regarding setting up each individual generating plant in the long run as well as hour-to-hour decisions on which generators to run for load sharing in the short run. The introduction of computer-controlled "dispatching" (or deciding on which generators to run during each time interval) has facilitated the coordination of plant operation on a continuing basis. Substantial economies, therefore, can be achieved with more intensive use of those plants that have lower marginal costs per kilowatt hour. In effect, such complete coordination in operation provides a larger choice of plants for generation in a descending order of priority based on per kilowatt hour marginal costs.

Stephen Breyer and Paul MacAvoy[6] discussed the effects of coordination on the production of electric power. They identified cost savings from effective coordination in six distinct categories,

(1) Operating costs: this can be achieved by more intensive operation of lower marginal cost plants, as mentioned earlier.

(2) Peak demand costs: since there may be seasonal or hourly differences in peak demand between two coordinating utilities, they could possibly share power with the off-peak area supplying power when the other area is experiencing peak demand. The peaking reserve provided in the two systems could be reduced considerably by such sharing, if the periods of peak demand on both are noncoincidental.

(3) Reserve costs: the extra kilowatt margin usually provided by utilities to allow for contingencies such as plant outages and unexpected increases in demand can be reduced by coordination, thereby reducing fixed costs associated with such reserve capacity.

(4) Generating costs: there are considerable economies of scale in plant size. As explained earlier the size of plant installed depends directly on the rate of growth in energy demand that the utility anticipates. When capacity planning is coordinated, the aggregate annual growth in kilowatt hours of two or more utilities would favor economically the adoption of larger plant sizes, with lower marginal costs per kilowatt hour.

(5) Transmission reliability costs: sudden start-ups and breakdowns of generating plants often result in heavy surges of current along transmission lines, which have to be "overdesigned" for such contingencies. This "overdesign" component of transmission costs can be reduced by coordination in planning of transmission lines.

(6) Social costs: since a larger geographic area served by two or more utilities offers more numerous locational choices, it is possible to confine the pollution associated with generating facilities to areas where the loss of social benefits is minimized. A smaller number of generating plants brought about by coordination in generation can also lead to lower social costs imposed by pollution.

The gains from coordination for a group of utilities would depend specifically on the seasonal patterns of demand experienced by them, the type of equipment employed, maintenance problems and outages encountered, and the spatial characteristics of their transmission and distribution systems. On a national scale, however, Breyer and MacAvoy calculate the potential gains from constructing larger plants at about 5 percent of newly installed capacity, or approximately $680 million annually. This along with other coordination-related savings, is estimated by the authors to lead to annual savings of $2.0 billion in 1980, that is, 3.5 percent of the total expected operating costs for that year.

In another detailed study, "Scale Frontiers in Electric Power,"[7] William R. Hughes found that all but a few of the largest power supply systems in the United States had encountered limitations in achieving economies of scale in generation. But a movement toward scale frontiers was observed with an increase in coordination between the smaller systems. The author concluded, however, that nuclear power technology could increase the scale-disparity between small systems on the one hand and large systems or groups of coordinated small systems on the other. This is likely because the economies of scale in nuclear power are more pronounced due to inherent scale economies in the reactor and heat exchange unit operation. The elasticity of costs with respect to unit size for nuclear plants was observed by Hughes to be about 0.7 for all sizes up to more than 3,000 Mw. The corresponding elasticity for large conventional steam plants installed in the 1960s was 0.9.

The Carolina Power and Light System is part of the Virginia-Carolinas Reliability Group (VACAR), of which the other members are Duke Power Company, Virginia Electric and Power Company, and four other smaller systems. Carolina Power and Light is also a member of the Southeastern Electric Reliability Council (SERC), an association consisting of 30 member companies whose purpose it is to increase system reliability for individual members. In mid-1974, the VACAR group had a reserve capacity of 16.4 percent over the reserves of individual members. The common reserve differs from one coordinating group to another and on the extent of dovetailing of plans actually followed by the members of a particular group.

Most power pools provide a "spinning"* reserve equal to the capacity of the largest generating unit available in the aggregated system. In some cases a further reserve also may be provided equal to the capacity of the second largest generating unit, though in this case the reserve unit may not be spinning but remain capable of generating power without a delay of longer than five to ten minutes. There are periods, of course, when this minimum reserve may be exceeded, as in the months and years immediately following the commissioning of a new plant, since new plants add to generating capacity in large blocks of kilowatts.

The benefits of coordination can be seen by reverting to the present value computations earlier in this chapter. It is conceivable that with the commitments to construction of excessively high generating capacities, most utilities would be in a position to sell power to neighboring regions over the next 10 to 12 years. Hence, let us assume that the VACAR group has enough capacity to take up the shortfall for Carolina Power and Light for the period 1984-87, enabling it to cancel the construction of the first nuclear plant in option (a). Then this would result in a reduction in present value of costs to $1,871,279.7, which makes it almost as economical as option (c).

It may seem somewhat puzzling that with such large economic benefits, the degree of coordination achieved in the electric power industry has not been greater than the record indicates. There are two main reasons for this. First, there are numerous managerial, accounting, and economic issues that make close coordination in planning and operation a complex problem. For instance, if there are two utilities, one of which has a poor maintenance and outage record and the other a good one, the provision of a common reserve then would be working mostly for the benefit of the former utility, and there could be disputes on whether the fixed costs of the reserve capacity should be borne equally by both or in proportion to the actual usage by each. Second, the relatively stable financial period that most utilities went through until 1972 inhibited an active change in the concept of individual planning and control toward coordination—the choices for financial growth were numerous and coordination was at the bottom of the list, with associated marginal benefits far smaller than the marginal costs of reorienting an established managerial structure. This has changed

---

*The term is used to indicate generators that are continuously kept running without any appreciable output of power—in readiness for taking on load whenever required by the system.

ECONOMICS OF ELECTRICITY SUPPLY 125

considerably, and particularly with the higher economies of scale of nuclear plants, coordination arrangements are likely to spread in the future, both in width and depth.

TRANSMISSION AND DISTRIBUTION COSTS

The provision of a suitable transmission and distribution system in a region is related intimately to the demand for electricity and the dispersal of generating capacity used in supplying power.

The transmission system in a region usually consists of such items as cables and lines (either overhead or underground); transformers and switchgears used at the terminals of transmission lines; and metering, relaying, and control systems for operating and protecting the transmission system. The most notable feature in transmission systems has been the movement toward higher voltages, known today as extra high voltage (EHV) transmission. The term EHV generally refers to voltages in the 230-KV (kilovolts) to 800-KV range, but the values that have been standardized are 230 KV, 345 KV, 500 KV, and 765 KV. The development of EHV is related to the fact that the capability of a transmission line increases roughly as the square of its rated voltage. This has acted as an incentive to technological development of higher rated voltages. As long as the additional cost in achieving higher voltages rises less rapidly than the transmission capability, there are obvious economies in EHV. This provides a rationale for expecting ultrahigh voltages (UHV) of over 800 KV in the future.

The most appropriate transmission system for a utility depends on a number of related features in the demand and supply characteristics of the region. The installation of EHV systems, therefore, has been brought about by economies of scale in generation that have resulted in large sources of power being concentrated in individual locations. There have been similar increases in concentration in areas of demand as well. Both these developments have resulted in the desirability of cheaper transmission of large quantities of energy over longer distances. The location of a number of "mine-mouth" generating plants away from consumption points also has led to the development of EHV transmission systems. Apart from transmission costs per kilowatt hour, EHV lines require lesser areas of land for a given quantity of energy transmitted, thereby reducing the cost of land for right-of-way and the problems associated with acquiring it.

The largest component of transmission costs is construction costs. The 1970 National Power Survey[8] gives the cost per mile of different types of conductors, all within the range of $77,400 to

$331,000. The average cost of 735-KV and 765-KV lines was $165,000 a mile, of which $18,700 was for right-of-way and clearing and the balance for construction costs. A 765-KV line requires approximately 200 feet of right-of-way, as compared with 750 feet for five 345-KV lines (which provide the same load-carrying capacity) and 3,000 feet for 138-KV lines with equivalent load capacity. There are, therefore, substantial economies in land costs with EHV systems.

Distribution systems again are related closely to the pattern of demand for electricity. Factors affecting changes in distribution costs over time are mainly (1) increasing load densities, (2) technological changes, (3) materials and labor costs, (4) cost of land, (5) cost of improving the appearance of facilities, and (6) cost of underground lines. Larger load densities usually result in lower costs since there are economies of scale in the cost of components in terms of dollars per unit capacity. This is essentially why utilities have declining block structures in their rate schedules. As in other areas of electricity supply, technological improvements in distribution equipment have led to substantial cost reductions.

The other factors mentioned above all contribute to cost increases, and this trend is likely to continue in the future. The main cost increase in distribution, however, is likely to take place due to one of these factors, namely, the cost of changing over to underground lines. In spite of these increases, the 1970 National Power Survey extrapolated costs of distribution for 1980 and 1990 as 0.431 cents per kilowatt hour and 0.375 cents per kilowatt hour, respectively, as against 0.523 cents per kilowatt hour in 1967. These costs are, however, sensitive to growth in demand; and current indications are that the cost reduction implicit in the above figures may not be realized as the growth in demand is lower than that envisaged by the FPC. It appears probable that with the prospect of lower future growth and greater financial difficulties, most utilities will slow down investments to eliminate overhead distribution lines, thereby being able to achieve, perhaps, a more modest decrease in distribution cost per kilowatt hour of energy sold than expected in the 1970 National Power Survey.

NOTES

1. Ralph Turvey, ed., Optimal Pricing and Investment in Electricity Supply (London, U.K.: Allen and Unwin, 1968), p. 12.
2. Federal Power Commission, The 1970 National Power Survey (Washington, D.C.: Government Printing Office, 1971) p. IV-1-73.
3. Seymour Baron, "Cost-Benefit Analysis of Advanced Power-Generation Methods," Energy Sources 1, no. 2 (winter 1974)

4. John N. Vernon, <u>Public Investment Planning in Civilian Nuclear Power</u> (Durham, N. C.: Duke University Press, 1971).

5. Policy Study Group of the MIT Energy Laboratory, "Energy Self Sufficiency: An Economic Evaluation," <u>Technology Review</u>, Cambridge, Mass.: MIT Press (May 1974).

6. Stephen G. Breyer and Paul W. MacAvoy, <u>Energy Regulation by the Federal Power Commission</u> (Washington, D. C.: The Brookings Institution, 1974).

7. William R. Hughes, "Scale Frontiers in Electric Power," <u>Technological Change in Regulated Industries,</u> William M. Capron, ed. (Washington, D. C.: The Brookings Institution, 1971).

8. Federal Power Commission, op. cit., p. IV-2-11.

CHAPTER

6

ELECTRIC UTILITY FINANCE

A recent article in <u>Financial World</u> was captioned "Electric Utilities—An Endangered Species;"[1] and the next line, in bold print, read, "Inability to cope with capital needs threatens industry's survival." A spate of comments, articles, and news analyses have appeared in various journals and magazines with similar headlines and titles. The provocation behind such headlines is a serious nationwide concern on the financial status of the investor-owned electric utility industry in the United States.

The financial operations of investor-owned utilities occupy a unique position in the market, mainly because of the fact that their rates are under the regulation of state agencies. Although these utilities have not suffered in the past from the regulatory process, with rapidly rising costs the lags usually observed in rate hearings and consequent revisions have imposed a serious constraint on their finances. The problem posed by regulation arises mainly from two facts. First, the process itself as it exists is time-consuming. Even if rate revisions are granted in full, the company has, in the meantime, built up a substantial negative balance in its accounts. Second, often the delays involved are so large that regulating commissions conclude a rate revision case with decisions based on data, which at the end of the process, are often up to two years old. This has compelled utilities over the nation to request further rate revisions while earlier requests are still pending with the regulators. The provision for automatic fuel price adjustment clauses in the regulation process has helped but not substantially altered the picture. Such clauses permit a utility to automatically pass on to customers, without any rate hearings, the full cost of any increases in the price of fuel. But with the recent escalation in interest and financing costs, construction costs, and wage bills, fuel costs generally have proved to be only one element in a variety of cost increases. Besides, fuel adjustment clauses, when invoked with great frequency, are regarded by customers as a betrayal by regulating commissions of the responsibility they are supposed to discharge on behalf of the region's electorate—an automatic adjustment is often regarded as a "give-away" to the utilities, who are sometimes visualized as exercising considerable power in the regulation of their own rate structures. The effects of such political sentiments cannot be minimized when charting the future of electric utilities in this country. The rapid rise in electric rates in the mid-1970s is not being questioned only by regulating commissions but also is inviting a strong and sometimes violent response from consumers. Early in 1975, under heavy pressure from an increasingly vocal and demonstrative public, the North Carolina Utilities Commission modified the automatic fuel adjustment clause applicable in the state to permit only 75 percent of fuel cost increases to be automatically passed on to customers. Faced with imperfections in the market for used goods, a consumer who has a given set of appliances and a home designed for extensive use of electricity has few immediate substitutes available at reasonable cost. Although adjustments in the long run would permit a less electricity-based lifestyle, rapid increases in the price of electricity in the short run will encourage consumers to take recourse to political or group action against those price increases that they perceive as offering them no immediate market choice. It would be politically naive to imagine that liberalization of regulation would permit electric utilities to increase prices to a point that would grant them financial stability. Such a view also ignores the resultant effects of large price increases on the long run demand for electrical energy, which would be against the interest of the industry itself as it is engaged in making heavy investments in future generating potential.

In expanding business, the electric utility industry has a number of sources from which to finance its construction and operation programs. The actual choice of a specific type of financing arrangement depends on (1) the condition of the securities markets, particularly in relation to a utility's own ranking therein, and (2) the desirability of maintaining a sound capital structure to keep the company attractive to investors in the future. Debt financing is usually the most attractive source of capital, but an increase in the debt-equity ratio for any company increases the extent of risk faced by its bondholders and the probability of fluctuations in earnings for stockholders. Such a development would reduce the attractiveness for investment in the company and increase future financing costs. Table 6.1 shows the capitalization ratios for all U.S. investor-owned electric utilities for the years 1966-73.

The long term debt ratio has remained fairly steady over the past few decades. It was 47.5 percent in 1937, 46.8 percent in 1947, 52.4

TABLE 6.1

Capitalization Ratios Expressed as Percentages—
All U.S. Investor Owned Electric Utilities

Year	1973	1972	1971	1970	1969	1968	1967	1966
Mortgage bonds	48.0	49.4	51.1	51.6	50.9	50.1	49.5	48.8
Other long term debt	4.9	4.3	3.6	3.7	4.1	4.0	3.8	3.7
Total long term debt	52.9	53.7	54.7	55.3	55.0	54.1	53.3	52.5
Preferred stock	12.0	11.7	10.7	9.8	9.5	9.6	9.7	9.5
Common stock equity	35.1	34.6	34.6	34.9	35.5	36.3	37.0	38.0
Total	100.0	100.0	100.0	100.0	100.0	100.0	100.0	100.0

Source: Edison Electric Institute, Statistical Year Book of the Electric Utility Industry for 1973 (New York: Edison Electric Institute, 1974).

TABLE 6.2

Weighted Average of Earnings
Moody's 24 Utility Common Stocks for 12 Months
Ending March 31
(in dollars per share)

Year	1974	1973	1972	1971	1970	1969	1968	1967	1966
Dollars per share	7.15	7.78	7.27	6.91	6.90	6.74	6.78	6.37	6.03

Source: Edison Electric Institute, Statistical Year Book of the Electric Utility Industry for 1973 (New York: Edison Electric Institute, 1974).

percent in 1957, and 52.4 percent in 1962. Most utilities also attempt to manage their finances so stockholders are assured of a fairly constant rate of annual earnings per share. This can be seen in the weighted average of earnings for the first quarters of the years 1966-74, shown in Table 6.2.

ELECTRIC UTILITY FINANCE   131

In normal years, utilities have performed well in maintaining steady earnings for stockholders. The problem has become acute since 1973 due to a large number of factors, some of which appeared much before the "energy crisis." Interest charges on debt, which were at an average of 4.5 percent in 1964, rose to 8.8 percent by 1970 for all new public utility bond issues. In June 1974 they had risen to 9.7 percent. These figures were referred to in a paper by Paul MacAvoy and Paul Joskow presented at the Annual Conference of the American Economic Association in December 1974[2]. The authors noted that the rate of return on equity, which had reached 12.8 percent in 1967, was 11.2 percent in 1973 and had gone down to 10.9 percent for the first nine months of 1974. Thus, the gap between the rate of return on equity and the interest on long term debt had all but vanished toward the end of 1974, making investments in electric utility stocks at par value an unattractive option. Even the earnings per share that have been realized are regarded with suspicion in the market because of a unique feature in the accounting practice generally followed by electric utilities. This arises out of the long term nature of commitment of funds necessary for construction in this industry.

Construction of generating and other facilities permits a utility to take into account an "allowance for funds used during construction" by offsetting the cost of funds tied up in constructing new plants and showing some amount from this as annual earnings. For instance, for every kilowatt of nuclear capacity being constructed at a cost of $500 it is possible to show $100 say, as earnings from this plant during the years of construction. While crediting the $100 to earnings in these years, a debit of $100 is raised against the capital costs of the plant, which in this case would amount to $600/Kw over the construction life of the plant. The rationale behind this accounting maneuver is to permit current stockholders an adequate return on capital that they have tied up in construction for long periods of time, although no actual cash flow of earnings takes place. This accounting practice is certainly not new, but an enlargement of its application to alarming proportions is a recent phenomenon. In 1965, this accounting practice provided approximately 5 percent of the electric utility industry's total profits. In 1974 the average figure was close to 35 percent, which raises serious questions about the "phoney" nature of these profits, particularly for those companies at the extreme end with 80 to 90 percent of their earnings from this allowance. Under these circumstances and with potential investors becoming aware of the extent of these "phantom profits" (as they often are called), it is doubtful if such practices could raise the value of electric utility stock in the market. The very objective for which they were designed will be defeated.

Another measure of financial desperation is seen in the rapidly spreading practice of "deferred fuel accounting." With frequent increases in fule prices cutting into utility profits, a number of companies have been postponing the inclusion of such price increases in their profit and loss accounts. This is achieved by not showing the higher costs until they have been recovered fully from customers, usually as a sequel to the application of automatic fuel adjustment clauses. The delay achieved in this manner often can add up to a year, during which period the company feels it is in a better position to attract financing without the inclusion of unrecovered fuel cost increases in its published accounts. Sooner or later, the legality of such accounting practices will have to stand the test of court challenges; some experts are doubtful of the outcome. Even the automatic fuel adjustment clause is regarded by some as illegal, and in Florida the state's attorney general has taken the position that the automatic adjustment clause is not legal.

A removal of the automatic fuel adjustment clause indeed would sound the death knell for a large number of investor-owned utilities. A recent congressional study estimates that in 1974 alone, the operation of such clauses resulted in an increases in total customer electric bills by approximately $6.5 billion. This increase in a single year is larger than the aggregate of all electric rate increases granted nationwide during the last 25 years. The extent of financial dependence by electric utilities on this adjustment provision can be seen from the fact that in spite of such a massive and rapid increase in customer bills, finances in this industry continue to be in a precarious state.

The question naturally arises: how do the utilities themselves propose to pull safely out of the current financial morass? There are, of course, the usual calls for financial help from the federal government in various forms, such as tax credits, guaranteed loans at low interest rates, and even direct subsidies. But the consensus most frequently voiced by utility executives consists of a total reform in the regulating process and elimination of the lags involved in rate increases. Richard Stinson[3] quotes Shearon Harris, president of Carolina Power and Light as saying, "I have grave concern that the regulatory process—which was never designed to cope with the degree and rate of change we've experienced recently—can respond adequately and expeditiously enough so as not to endanger the power supply of the nation." But one may add, with some insight, that the management of electric utilities, too, was never designed to cope with the degree and rate of change experienced since 1974. Most executives perceive the slowdown in growth of demand as a result of their own conservation efforts and only nominally as a price-related phenomenon. They are also, by and large, in blissful ignorance of the lagged nature of changes in quantity demanded in response to changes in price of electricity. In the same article, Donald C. Cook, chairman of American Electric

Power, has been quoted as thinking that "rate boosts of 20 percent t0 25 percent every year or so to produce profits sufficient to meet capital needs" are required. This would mean a doubling of electricity prices about every three years, and the effect in the long run is likely to be a sharp cutback in demand for electricity—making redundant the very capacity such drastic rate increases are designed to finance. The interaction of the financial needs of an electric utility with the demand for electrical energy by its customers and the utility's capacity to supply power are examined in detail in Part III of this book.

For an industry going through financial difficulties, the handicaps it faces run full circle when its bonds or stocks are downgraded in the market. A large number of electric utilities have been victims of such a series of developments, including Carolina Power and Light. Early in 1975, that utility's long range bonds were downgraded by Moody's Investors Service from A to Baa rating. This action usually is taken as a result of or in anticipation of financial difficulties for the company. However, the action itself triggers off a deterioration in the company's finances as a result of an increase in the cost of borrowing. Table 6.3 shows the average yield on A and Baa rated bonds, respectively, for the last twelve quarters for the entire United States.

It can be seen from these figures that the difference in yields on these two types of bonds has been as much as 0.60 percent in some quarters. Most analysts feel that the downgrading of Carolina Power and Light bonds will result in approximately a 0.5 percent increase in the cost of long term borrowing, which will further compound its capital-related financial difficulties. This must be viewed in conjunction with the fact that the investment climate is nervous, and most portfolio managers tend to be extremely quality-conscious in such a climate. Many of them have been avoiding even AA rated electric utility bonds, and most of them are eliminating A bonds because a number of utilities in addition to Carolina Power and Light have had their A rating reduced to Baa. In fact, from January to October 1974, a total of 21 bond ratings for utilities were downgraded by Moody's; and only two were upgraded. For most of these utilities the downgrading meant that bond issues carrying approximately 8.5 percent yields in January 1974 now would require effective yields of around 11 percent. This amounts to an increase in cost of capital of over 25 percent in less than a year.

The conclusion reached when confronted with such high costs of long term debt financing and the difficulty in selling bonds in an indifferent market is that perhaps the utilities should float additional issues of common stock. Unfortunately, the prospect for this option, too, is grim. The average price of common stocks of the 50 largest electric utilities at the end of 1974 was about 60 percent of book value. This makes the issue of common stock at such low prices a shortsighted action, since such offerings would lead to a dilution of earnings per

TABLE 6.3

Average Yields on Moody's A and Baa Rated Bonds
(in percent)

	Yearly Quarters			
	1st	2nd	3rd	4th
1971				
A	7.99	8.45	8.23	7.80
Baa	8.59	8.77	8.45	8.40
1972				
A	7.76	7.80	7.64	7.51
Baa	8.25	8.30	7.96	7.74
1973				
A	7.69	7.78	8.08	8.24
Baa	8.01	7.97	8.52	8.59

Source: Edison Electric Institute, Statistical Year Book of the Electric Utility Industry for 1973 (New York: Edison Electric Institute, 1974).

share, reducing even further the value of future stocks to be offered by the company.

If the scenario presented above appears grim, such an impression is correct. The situation, however, can be called desperate but not hopeless. Hope lies in bold action by government and industry. The links in the system require such action to be confined not only to direct efforts at financing but also to changing investment plans. Some policies aimed at improving electric utility finances are examined in Part III.

NOTES

1. Richard J. Stinson, "Electric Utilities—an Endangered Species," Financial World (January 9, 1975).
2. Paul Joskow, and Paul W. MacAvoy, "Shifts in the Electric Power Industry," paper presented at the Allied Social Science Association's Annual Meeting at San Francisco, December 1974.
3. Stinson, op. cit.

PART III
POLICY ALTERNATIVES FOR THE FUTURE

INTRODUCTION TO PART III

Up to this point some important factors have been discussed that individually affect the demand for electrical energy on the one hand; and the ability of an electric utility to supply power on the other. The link between these two appears in the form of plans for additions in generating capacity, based on the utility's perception of demand in the future. This link extends further into the financial operations of the utility, making the ability to invest in future supply potential dependent on the ability to finance investments, both through internal savings and external means. In Part III, this link will be quantified by extending the model developed in the previous chapters. This will then be used as a framework for examining certain policy alternatives that would affect demand as well as supply in the electric utility industry. By studying the detailed micromodel of one of the leading electric utilities in the nation, one will be able to draw relevant conclusions on what policies could be adopted for the nation as a whole.

In the crisis atmosphere enveloping the future of electric utilities in this country, it is easy and tempting to come up with instant solutions. One-sentence "gems" of wisdom are becoming commonplace. Some of these solutions have considerable merit; some others ignore the feedback effects and dynamic links in the system that they are supposed to rejuvenate. Part III examines some of these solutions explicitly and lays a basis for evaluation of other possible actions.

CHAPTER

7

INTERACTIONS BETWEEN SUPPLY AND DEMAND

To formulate and implement a suitable investment plan a utility requires (1) information on future energy demand, both in nature and magnitude; (2) the costs of components that constitute each alternative in power generation; and (3) adequate financing to fund the investment program. Whereas improvements in forecasting methodology bring qualitative improvements in the first of these requirements within the control of a utility, there is not much that it can do with regard to the second. The main area toward which company policies and enlightened management are directed, often with considerable impact, is the area of financing. Financing of new investments has become a crucial problem for the electric utility industry, as explained in Chapter 10; and this is likely to remain so in the future when capital-intensive nuclear expansion continues.

In this chapter the dynamic model will be extended to provide computations of some financial variables, thereby enabling an appraisal of the capital-related problems within the industry in a dynamic setting. One reason for such an analysis is to foresee the effects of policies that call for drastic increases in price for a number of years to provide adequate internally generated funds for financing. Proponents of this view rightly contend that large price increases will in the short run lead to higher earnings and attract external funds to the industry, but wrongly assume that such price increases will have no effect on demand in the long run.

The first exercise in extending the model was to include a cost function. This was done by adopting a set of simplifying assumptions.

(1) Total operating costs were divided into two components—a fixed cost per kilowatt of generating capacity and a variable operating cost per kilowatt hour of energy generated.

SUPPLY AND DEMAND INTERACTIONS   139

(2) The fixed cost component was estimated from past data for the specific Carolina region by excluding fuel costs from total expenses but adding interest charges for each of the years 1968-73. These figures were than divided by the existing capacity in megawatts for each year, respectively. The values of costs per megawatt thus obtained were divided by the consumer price index to express them in real terms in line with all other costs and prices used in the model. These real values for the years 1968-73 were $31.47, $31.226, $29.42, $29.05, $30.192, and $29.47 thousand, respectively. The average of these values, $29.80 thousand, was the fixed cost per kilowatt in the dynamic model. In other words, fixed costs per kilowatt were assumed to remain unchanged in the future. It was felt the sacrifice of specificity in using this assumption was not serious enough to warrant a more detailed set of formulations relating interest charges, wages, maintenance charges, taxes, and so on to the actual break-up of capacity into its nuclear, fossil-fuel, and ICTG components. Thus, to obtain total fixed operating costs for any future period, the model merely multiplies total capacity existing in megawatts by 29.80 ÷ 6 (because the unit time interval used for simulation is two months, or one-sixth of a year).

(3) The variable cost component used related only to fuel costs. These were included as the product of average cost of fuels per British thermal unit and British thermal unit per kilowatt hour used in generation. The figures used in the model were extracted from the Edison Electric Institute's Year Book for 1973, which gives the weighted average cost per British thermal unit of all the fuels used in generating electricity during the year.

The assumptions mentioned above might appear generalized and inflexible. There were two reasons for their adoption and use in the model. First, it is difficult at this stage to assess how prices of all inputs in general and fuel prices in particular are going to vary in the future. The most accurate way to model these would be to include stochastic effects on price movements, an accurate estimate of global factors affecting prices in the United States, and forecasts of technological changes and economies of scale in the future. This would not only have been beyond the scope of the present study but also could have been deficient in reliability if at all attempted. Second, the assumption of constant real costs explained above is perhaps optimistic from a utility's point of view; and this suited the study's approach since it intended to explore various policies and their effects, given the most favorable sets of conditions in supply costs.

Since generating capacity is a determinant of operating costs and is itself the result of investments made, when one is exploring the utility's financing possibilities this variable has to be included in the dynamic model. As a starting point, the generating capacities to be established in the future were entered in accordance with the utility's expansion plans as they stood during 1974. These plans are undergoing intensive reappraisal and before the year 1975 is out may have been modified substantially. As such the schedule shown for commissioning of new plants may be considered as being only a starting point in the analysis, a tentative schedule that will continue to be revised by the company in years to come.

Table 7.1 shows the elements of this capacity addition program. In this table only the years of completion against each plant have been shown, but in the model itself the information that was available to make these effective from the precise months for which completion is scheduled was used in the case of plants in the near future.

TABLE 7.1

Data on Future Capacity Addition Plan for
the Carolina Power and Light System

Year	Plant Capacity (in megawatts)	Type	Cumulative Capacity (in megawatts)
1974	821	Nuclear	6815.5
1975	821	Nuclear	7636.5
1977	720	Fossil	8356.5
1979	1,150	Fossil	9506.5
1979	900	Nuclear	10406.5
1980	900	Nuclear	11306.5
1981	900	Nuclear	12206.5
1982	900	Nulcear	13106.5
1983	1,150	Nuclear	14256.5
1984	1,150	Nuclear	15406.5
1985	1,150	Nuclear	16556.5
1985	1,150	Nuclear	17706.5
1986	900	Nuclear	18606.5
1987	1,150	Nuclear	19756.5
1988	1,150	Nuclear	20906.5
1989	1,150	Nuclear	22056.5
1990	900	Nuclear	22956.5
1991	1,150	Nuclear	24106.5
1992	1,150	Nuclear	25256.5

Source: Compiled by author.

The model was then run simulating the period up to 1990 to provide forecasts of net revenue inclusive of dividends on the basis of cost assumptions explained above. These revenues were the difference between operating revenues and operating costs, capital expenditures being excluded from the computation. Total revenues were computed by the model, directly using the average price per kilowatt hour for each group and the total electricity consumed by the particular group in kilowatt hours.

At this stage an addition was also made to the model to take account of seasonal variations in demand, since this would give a more accurate assessment of peaking loads in the future and possibly more reliable forecasts of revenue, which naturally fluctuate from month to month with demand. Seasonal effects were incorporated in the model by using electricity consumption data for the region for the years 1965-73. Consumption for all separate sectors modeled were aggregated by two-month intervals for this period. This was then adjusted for the mean rate of growth to separate out changes between periods that did not relate to seasonal factors. The ratio of each two-month value to the adjusted average for the year was then calculated. For instance, these ratios for the high consumption rate group in the residential sector were 0.772, 1.08, 1.594, 1.35, 0.705, and 0.79—the first of these values being for the July-August period and the last for the May-June period.

The different sets of values obtained were then used as inputs to the model for the three individual rate groups in the residential sector, for each subsector in the commercial sector, and for the industrial sector as a whole. The value of kilowatt hour per customer in the former two sectors and kilowatt hour per dollar of value added in the industrial sector, computed as before in the model, is then multiplied by the appropriate seasonal ratio in each case. Simulation runs were then carried out employing these effects up to 1990.

The effect of seasonal factors is included in the factors computed for megawatt capacity required as shown in Table 7.2. The capacity required during a particular period was determined by selecting the highest two-month peak in energy demand during the year, calculating the megawatt capacity required to meet this load at 60 percent load factor, and adding on a 13 percent reserve. This was done in recognition of the concern expressed by utility officials that with higher energy demands in the future, the absolute peaks in between months would continue to increase requiring higher capacity additions than warranted by annual energy figures alone. Alongside this column in Table 7.2 is shown the megawatt capacity that would be available if the 1974 capacity addition program were to be followed in the Carolina region.

142   ELECTRICAL SUPPLY AND DEMAND

TABLE 7.2

Interaction Between Demand,
Investment Planning, and Financial Status

Year	Capacity Required	Capacity Planned (in megawatts)	Capacity Required (in thousands of dollars)	Net Earnings (in thousands of dollars)	Net Earnings ÷ Capital Required
1975	5572.6	7636.5	518,665	228,200	0.4399
1976	5637.1	8356.5	493,758	228,900	0.4636
1977	5766.1	9506.5	564,750	239,500	0.4241
1978	5882.2	10406.5	715,625	235,700	0.3294
1979	5675.8	11306.5	846,367	221,900	0.2622
1980	5753.2	12206.5	978,900	226,000	0.2309
1981	5908.0	13106.5	981,942	237,300	0.2417
1982	6088.6	14256.5	1,008,900	251,100	0.2489
1983	6282.1	15406.5	1,054,567	270,500	0.2565
1984	6488.5	16556.5	1,041,725	297,300	0.2854
1985	6707.8	17706.5	1,085,608	327,100	0.3013
1986	6965.8	18606.5	822,867	352,400	0.3246*
1987	7326.9	19756.5	843,242	390,000	0.3592*
1988	7713.9	20906.5	712,333	445,500	0.4104*
1989	8152.6	22056.5	581,425	519,300	0.4783*
1990	8668.5	22956.5	431,767	615,200	0.5667*

*Ratios calculated with values of capital required assumed to remain unchanged from the 1985 level of $1,085,608,000.

Note: In calculating capital required it has been assumed that construction expenditures on transmission and distribution in the future remain in the same ratio to investments in generating capacity as they are at present. The figures in the third column include expected investments on transmission and distribution facilities.

Source: Compiled by the author.

The other columns in Table 7.2 show the capital expenditure financing requirements of the utility and the net earnings (inclusive of dividends) of the utility. The financing requirements were calculated by assuming the same timing of cash flows and costs as used in Chapter 5, both for nuclear and fossil-fuel based generating plants. Since the expansion plan ends with the plants to be commissioned in 1992, there is a decline in financing requirements beyond 1986. This

SUPPLY AND DEMAND INTERACTIONS   143

is misleading, because even if a utility has no specific investment plans beyond 1992, it would attempt to plan for financing at least at the same level as the 1985 requirement. Net earnings are computed as mentioned before. The figures in Table 7.2 have all been computed with the uniform growth in price assumptions of 5.52 percent used before.

The last two columns in Table 7.2 provide an interesting forecast of the electric utility industry's financial health. Whereas the capital required to finance the tentative capacity addition program keeps on increasing steadily throughout the period (assuming a continuation of plant additions beyond 1992), the net revenues generated within the utility show no fixed trend. There is first a slow increase up to 1977, and then a decline in 1978 and 1979; but beyond 1979 an increasing trend sets in that accelerates through 1990. Corresponding ratios of net earnings to total capital required similarly decrease from 0.4399 in 1975 to a low of 0.2309 in 1980. Beyond this year, however, this ratio increases steadily to 0.3013 in 1985 and further to 0.5667 in 1990 (with the assumptions underlying this variable for the years 1986-90).

The inferences to be drawn from these computed values are mainly that the capital requirements of the industry will continue to be far in excess of internal financing capabilities for the next five or six years and that expansion programs originally drawn up will have to be drastically cut if the industry is to survive. The longer term view is, however, not so dismal. With the current outlook for decisions to reduce investments, it is obviously possible to scale down capital requirements substantially, at least from 1983-84. This would restore the ability of the industry to finance most of its future expansion, increase earnings per share, and, therefore, also attract external financing at lower costs.

The crucial assumptions in these computations are in regard to capital costs, generating costs, and prices of electricity over the time span simulated. The deficiency in information regarding future costs and the fact that these are usually not within the control of a utility make the cost assumptions used a matter of expediency, if not of accuracy. However, electricity prices are, to a large extent, within the control of policy makers in government and industry. Hence, it would be useful to study the effects of different prices on the financial future of the electric utility industry. This was done in a series of computer runs in which three rates of price increases were used.

	Two-Month Rate of Real Growth in Price of			
	Electricity	Gas	Coal	Fuel Oil
Pricing scheme A	0.9%	1.7%	0.9%	1.7%
Pricing scheme B	1.8%	1.7%	0.9%	1.7%
Pricing scheme C	2.7%	1.7%	0.9%	1.7%

The first of these schemes used the same price increases that were used in some simulation runs in Part I. Schemes B and C were experimented with to assess the long run dynamic effects of steep increases in electricity prices in accordance with views often aired by industry officials such as Donald C. Cook, chairman of American Electric Power.[1] Scheme C is equivalent to a real rate of annual increase in electricity prices of 17.33 percent. In a single year such a large increase may not have much significance, but if sustained over 16 years up to 1990, this would amount to a total real increase of 259.15 percent over the level of prices existing in 1974.

We have presented in Table 7.3 the results from these simulation runs only for the years 1975, 1978, 1981, 1984, 1987, and 1990. The capital required is in keeping with the Carolina Power and Light capacity addition plan detailed earlier and remains the same with price assumption A, B, or C. The last column showing total energy demand in million kilowatt hours was included to relate the utility's financial results with the corresponding effect on energy demand in each case.

The results of the three simulation runs show a marked improvement in the finances of the utility with steeper price increases. At first glance this seems paradoxical, because with electric energy demand being elastic in the long run, price increases, it appears, should not increase revenues in the long run. The reason for increased revenues, however, is that although prices are acting toward reducing demand, incomes and time-related trends affect demand in the other direction, negating part of the price effect. At any rate, the overall price elasticity for the aggregate of all residential, industrial, and commercial demand is probably close to unity, thus having a minor price-related effect on revenues. The combined effect of all these factors, then, is to increase revenues and net earnings in the long run.

The interrelationship between supply and demand, however, is brought out by examining the values for total energy demand in relation to the financial picture for each year. Price assumption A clearly does not ameliorate the financial condition of the utility—our 1981 value for the key net earnings ratio reaching a low of 0.2672. Energy demand with this price assumption increases steadily over the entire period, the 1990 value being 87.2 percent higher than the 1975 value. However, the capacity built up with this plan does not reach a level of full utilization. With price assumption B, demand declines approximately 1.5 percent in the period 1975-78 and 7.8 percent between 1978-81, and then remains more or less stable during the remainder of the period up to 1990.

Price assumption C shows a marked difference in results obtained as against those from A and B. Demand in this case reduces nominally from 1975-78, but thereafter continues to plunge lower at a rapid rate; so in 1990 demand actually reaches a value 58.4 percent

TABLE 7.3

Effect of Varying Electricity Prices on
Future Financial Operations of the Utility

Price Assumption	Year	Capital Required (in thousands of dollars)	Net Earnings (in thousands of dollars)	Net Earnings ÷ Capital Required	Total Energy Demand (in million KwH)
A	1975	518,665	228,600	0.4407	2,513
	1978	715,625	243,700	0.3405	2,682
	1981	981,942	262,400	0.2672	2,890
	1984	1,041,725	351,400	0.3373	3,318
	1987	1,085,608	490,600	0.4519	3,886
	1990	1,085,608	789,000	0.7268	4,705
B	1975	518,665	244,400	0.4712	2,500
	1978	715,625	347,300	0.4853	2,462
	1981	981,942	423,900	0.4317	2,270
	1984	1,041,725	578,700	0.5555	2,187
	1987	1,085,608	813,000	0.7489	2,153
	1990	1,085,608	1,256,000	1.1570	2,197
C	1975	518,665	260,400	0.5021	2,482
	1978	715,625	464,600	0.6492	2,276
	1981	981,942	597,100	0.6081	1,798
	1984	1,041,725	796,000	0.7641	1,452
	1987	1,085,608	1,081,000	0.9968	1,200
	1990	1,085,608	1,597,000	1.4711	1,032

Source: Compiled by author.

lower than the 1975 value. It is obvious that steep increases in electricity prices will result in significant improvements in the finances of the electric utility in the long run, but this would be accompanied by drastic reductions in the consumption of electrical energy. On a political plane such an effect, it seems, will not be acceptable in any region of the country. It is unlikely that households, commercial establishments, and industries will either be able to bring about such a large shift to consumption of substitutes for electricity without serious dislocations in the nation's economy.

In carrying out the above computations we have used a set of assumptions favorable to the financial health of the electric utility industry. We have assumed generating and construction costs to remain unchanged in real terms up to 1990, an objective which is perhaps attainable but not likely. Further, the prices of fuel oil and natural gas have been assumed to be high for all three sectors, leading to a higher long run demand for electricity. The conclusion then is that the finances of the industry would remain perhaps in a state somewhat worse than that indicated by the results from each simulation run. Price increases cannot therefore be relied on as the only means to alleviate the current financial problems of electric utilities even with the most favorable sets of exogenous conditions. The most practical step to take, it appears, is to reduce capital requirements through large cutbacks in expansion plans for the future. This may involve large losses if plants scheduled for the immediate future are cancelled, but it may yet be possible to put back or cancel at least those plants scheduled for completeion in 1982 or beyond without adverse financial effects.

The tentative Carolina Power and Light schedule in 1974 called for the construction of 12 generating plants in the period 1982-92, totaling 13,050 Mw in capacity. If these plants were to be cancelled, the utility would still have 12206.5 Mw of capacity in 1982, capable of generating 6415.74 billion KwH of energy at 60 percent load factor. This would be well above the demand projections with our model, using any of the sets of prices assumed in the computer runs described above. With these cancellations financing requirements for the period 1975-81 will be reduced considerably to annual values of 465,082; 400,050; 359,100; 373,475; 374,850; 272,400; and 169,950 (in thousands of dollars) for each of the seven years, respectively. Such a revision of plans would, therefore, make the financing of new capacity additions possible through internal savings and normal external sources. The financial crisis in the industry then merely becomes a temporary problem, and knowledge of this fact would definitely be revealed in stock market behavior. If investors are aware of the potential long run improvement in the financial health of the industry, investments would be forthcoming at lower costs than currently prevailing.

There is little doubt that in actual fact the cutbacks in new construction indicated above will be made by the industry, but the realization of slowing growth in demand probably will take four or five years. In this period only gradual trimming of future investments will be envisaged, and the atmosphere of financial fright is likely to continue. It is understandable that the electric utilities of the United States, being institutionally responsible for supplying power wherever and whenever demanded in their respective regions, would be hesitant to take drastic decisions affecting future generating capacity. The dynamic interactions between factors relating demand and supply in the electrical energy sector as presented in this chapter imply strongly that forces and trends have set in that can only be controlled through a careful set of pricing and investment policies to be formulated by the electric utility industry. In any action taken to ensure future supply of electric power, the effect on demand necessarily must be noted, as well as the other way around. These effects are not always obvious due to the nature of lags relating prices and incomes to demand and those relating financial investments to generating capacity and supply. The material contained in this chapter has been presented with a view to exposing some of these less obvious interrelationships.

NOTES

1. Richard J. Stinson, "Electric Utilities—an Endangered Species," Financial World (January 8, 1975).

CHAPTER

8

THE RESTRUCTURING OF ELECTRIC RATES

The 1974-75 spate of price increases in electricity has brought the subject of rate structures to the fore in public debates on the energy crisis. Electric utility rate economics is a vast area in which numerous books have been written and much detailed research conducted. In the presentation here, only those broad aspects of rate economics will be detailed that would affect public policy in rate making and its related impact on the electrical energy sector of the U.S. economy.

Most electric utilities in the United States have been following a system of declining block rates, which have the effect of reducing the average cost of electricity per unit as a customer buys larger and larger quantities. In a period of steadily declining relative prices of electricity this aspect of rates did not spark serious controversy on this continent, but issues of equity related to rate structures are now receiving more serious attention. However, the consequences of a utility's choice of certain rate structures are much wider. Rate structures must provide, as in the case of any pricing scheme, a vehicle for promoting economic efficiency. The considerations involved in using efficiency criteria are rather complex, on account of economies of scale in generation and the necessity for taking into account the peak-load characteristics of demand. Some components of electric utility rate economics are briefly described in the following paragraphs.

An efficient and equitable rate structure must be designed to recover from a customer the full costs of supplying power. These costs are usually considered as falling into three categories.

(1) Customer costs: these costs include those administrative costs involved in reading meters, processing accounts, and billing and the investment cost of meters and certain other parts of electric

plants. These costs are usually of a fixed nature and are incurred whether or not any power is consumed.

(2) Fixed costs: these consist of investment costs apportioned on the basis of electric plant usage as it is allocated to each customer. This would include fixed costs associated with distribution lines, substations, transmission lines, and generating plant. These costs are proportional, as described earlier, to the maximum demand in kilowatts that a particular customer places on the system. Peak loads and seasonal demands are, therefore, of direct relevance to the estimation of fixed costs.

(3) Variable costs: these costs are essentially energy costs including all components of operating costs, which vary directly with the amount of energy produced in kilowatt hours. The largest component of variable costs is the cost of fuel burned in power generation.

Given perfect information and costless measurement of load imposed and electricity consumed by each customer at all times during the year, it would be possible to apportion the above costs to each customer precisely for exact recovery. However, since the cost of metering to measure load (kilowatts) and energy (kilowatt hours) historically has been high, it has not been economically justifiable for certain categories of relatively small customers to be billed for consumption on the basis of all these cost measures. As a feasible alternative, pricing has been implemented using "declining block" schedules, which are designed to recover, as precisely as possible, all customer costs and most of the fixed costs in the first price blocks facing a customer. Successive blocks are designed in declining steps to reflect the reduction in customer and fixed costs per kilowatt hour as consumption of energy keeps on increasing. The last block is designed to recover primarily the variable costs per kilowatt hour in generation. A minimum bill is usually specified to ensure recovery of customer costs, even if no energy is consumed.

For large industrial customers, precise billing based on meters recording load in kilowatts and energy in kilowatt hours is justified. Hence, such customers are usually billed separately in a two-part bill. A special feature of rates designed for such customers is the provision of the ratchet clause. Under this clause, large industrial customers pay for a certain percentage of their maximum kilowatt load to cover the investment costs made by the utility to build up its generating capacity, even if the maximum load used by the customer in a particular month is lower. The actual magnitude of costs recovered through the application of the ratchet clause varies from region to region. Usually the minimum load included for purposes of billing varies from 50 to 100 percent. The quantity of energy consumed in kilowatt hours is billed in addition to the above charge and is generally based on a flat price per kilowatt hour.

Two other factors are now being given greater consideration in rate design—the increasing costs of pollution control and the seasonal nature of some types of load, both of which increase total fixed costs for a utility. Emphasis increasingly is being placed on the importance of regarding long run incremental costs as the only rational basis for pricing electricity. The era of across-the-board rate increases now seems over, due to the realization that static rate structures not related to long run incremental costs encourage unwarranted growth of a utility's rate base. Further, with some customers paying less than the full cost of power, any increase in sales to them will allow earnings attrition to continue for the utility, thereby hampering its ability to meet its responsibilities. If these responsibilities are viewed in a static single-period setting, electric-utility rates would appear to have a narrow effect. A long run view, however, would reveal the importance of rates in promoting different forms of electric consumption in the future. These rates, in turn, would inclilence the investment plans of the utility and directly affect total fixed costs in the future. In a situation of severe financial constraints, the industry and its regulators necessarily must direct their policies toward meeting their responsibilities in the long run.

In this particular study, the author has not gone into the allocation of various costs of supplying electrical energy to different customers. Other than the general principles mentioned above, there is little that can be said unless a specific set of rates pertaining to a particular utility is to be investigated. This investigation was aimed at estimating the extent to which changes in electric rates can affect the future operations of the electric utility industry. In doing this, an attempt has been made to shift some of the fixed costs of supplying power to groups of customers who are possibly at present being cross-subsidized by other groups of customers, in the opinions of rate economics experts.

The first series of simulations were carried out with regard to reducing seasonal peaks in energy demand. To the extent that a customer demands a higher amount of energy than his average during a particular season during the year, he is requiring the utility concerned to set up supply capacity that is used fully only during the periods of peak demand and remains unutilized or underutilized during the remainder of the year. The provision of such capacity adds to the system's fixed costs, which if not correctly imposed on the seasonal demand customer, would promote cross-subsidization by other customers who may have a more steady demand pattern and also would result in economic inefficiency by encouraging unwarranted increases in seasonal demands in the long run. The intention of this particular exercise was, therefore, to determine how the imposition of higher costs related to seasonal demand would affect long run fixed costs for the entire system. This was done by introducing a system of seasonally fluctuating prices. As explained in the previous chapter, the dynamic model used in this study was expanded to include seasonal variations in demand. It was proposed to counter this seasonal pattern by devising prices that would be higher in the months when demand usually peaked and lower when it typically declined.

The base simulation run made for comparison used the earlier assumption of electricity, fuel oil, coal, and natural gas prices growing at a real rate of 5.52 percent annually. The values obtained with this assumption were computed and plotted, and the output thus obtained. The next run was made by assuming, in addition to the equivalent 5.52 percent annual increase in prices, a superimposed pattern of seasonal increases (Pricing scheme A), which varied in the following ratio: July-August–1.05; September-October–1.05; November-December–1.00; January-February–1.00; March-April–0.95; May-June–1.00. A third run was made with a slightly larger seasonal difference in prices (Pricing scheme B), which was again superimposed on the annual increase rate of 5.52 percent. This difference was in the following ratio: July-August–0.075; September-October–1.075; November-December–1.00; January-February–1.075; March-April–0.95; May-June–1.00.

To estimate the long run effects on demand using these seasonal pricing schemes, we have retained our original nine-year inverted-V lag structure. In this situation, nevertheless, the adjustment in quantity demanded related to the differential price between two-month periods shows up once a year, when that particular time interval (DT) is being simulated. In the absence of advance information, the difference in price between two successive intervals would bring about a single-period adjustment in quantity demanded by a small amount, in accordance with the lag-structure assumed. With advance knowledge of seasonal price differentials, however, a consumer would be adjusting his stock of appliances and pattern of demand continuously, even during periods when the differential does not apply. In practical terms, if consumers are aware in, say, the summer of 1975 that electricity prices in the summer of 1976 will be higher than in other months, they would move in the direction of perhaps installing better insulation and buying lower capacity and more efficient air-conditioners. In effect, the total response to seasonal price differentials between yearly intervals would correspond to the cumulative full year response represented by the appropriate portion of the nine-year lag structure.

In the computer program itself, the seasonal pricing cycle is used by calling subroutine CBOX as developed in FORDYN.[1] In the simulations carried out as described above, the seasonal pricing scheme commenced with January-February 1975 and continued its application through the entire period terminating in 1990. The total

TABLE 8.1

Effect of Seasonal Pricing

Year and Period	No Seasonal Pricing Demand (in billion KwH)	Deviation from peak demand	Pricing Scheme A Demand (in billion KwH)	Deviation From Peak Demand	Pricing Scheme B Demand (in billion KwH)	Deviation From Peak Demand
1980 1	4.11	-0.30	4.20	-0.19	4.24	-0.22
2	4.21	-0.10	4.41	0	<u>4.46</u>	0
3	4.17	-0.24	4.34	-0.07	<u>4.39</u>	-0.07
4	4.25	-0.16	4.33	-0.08	4.37	-0.09
5	<u>4.41</u>	0	4.40	-0.01	4.39	-0.07
6	4.36	-0.05	4.35	-0.05	4.34	-0.12
Total	25.61	-0.85	26.03	-0.40	26.19	-0.55
1985 1	4.90	-0.44	4.95	-0.31	4.96	-0.25
2	5.14	-0.20	5.19	-0.07	5.20	-0.01
3	4.99	-0.35	5.15	-0.11	5.16	-0.05
4	5.12	-0.22	5.16	-0.10	5.17	-0.04
5	<u>5.34</u>	0	<u>5.26</u>	0	<u>5.21</u>	0
6	5.28	-0.06	5.20	-0.06	5.15	-0.06
Total	30.77	-1.27	30.91	-0.65	30.85	-0.41
1990 1	6.35	-0.73	6.32	-0.54	6.28	-0.44
2	6.58	-0.50	6.55	-0.31	6.51	-0.21
3	6.43	-0.65	6.56	-0.30	6.52	-0.20
4	6.70	-0.38	6.66	-0.20	6.62	-0.10
5	<u>7.08</u>	0	<u>6.86</u>	0	<u>6.72</u>	0
6	7.03	-0.05	6.80	-0.06	6.66	-0.06
Total	40.17	-2.31	39.75	-1.41	39.31	-1.01

Note: The peak energy demand for a two-month interval during each year has been underlined.
Source: Compiled by author.

long run response in quantity demanded consequently was completed nine years later by 1984 and continued at the same level thereafter.

Table 8.1 shows the effects of implementing these two seasonal pricing schemes. The results shown are for the three selected years 1980, 1985, and 1990, the values appearing in this table being for the two-month intervals for each of these three years.

The effects of introducing seasonal pricing are brought out clearly by observing the deviations from the peak two-month energy demand for each of these years. With scheme A, the peak demand remains at 4.41 billion kilowatt hours but shifts to March-April 1985 from September-October 1985. The deviations from the peaks for each DT, however, are reduced considerably as revealed by the total of -0.40 for 1985 as against -0.85 without the seasonal pricing scheme. This effect is reinforced in magnitude in 1985 and 1990. The long run results obtained from pricing scheme B are even more desirable. In this case the total deviations from the peak for 1980 are larger than those obtained with scheme A, but the results for 1985 and 1990 are much better. In 1985 the total deviations change to -0.41 and in 1990 to -1.01, both of which are considerably lower than those obtained from pricing scheme A.

It is evident from these results that a seasonal pricing scheme would have significant financial benefits to the utility and, consequently, to its customers. The reduction in peak energy demand is achieved without any significant drop in total annual demand; in other words, seasonal pricing would flatten out energy demanded over the yearly cycle. To assess the financial impact of this effect one need only consider the peak demand for 1990 achieved with scheme B. If the provision of capacity is based on a 60 percent load factor for the system with a 13 percent reserve, the reduction in peak demand during 1990 would itself warrant a reduction of 77.397 Mw of generating capacity. With the fixed cost assumption used in the model, this would amount to a reduction of $2.3 million in fixed costs alone for the year, not considering explicitly the costs of construction of generating plants to provide this additional capacity.

Seasonal pricing schemes have been used with considerable success in other countries and their adoption in the United States, would, at this stage, be justified on a number of grounds. Realizing this the Federal Energy Administration (FEA) has been working closely with the Vermont Public Utilities Commission and the Green Mountain Power Company to test the effects of various prices during the peak load winter season.

The increase in capital costs with the introduction of nuclear plants has led to another aspect of rate structures used in pricing electricity. The contention now being made is that declining blocks currently in use were designed during periods when capital costs were lower. Additional energy demands in kilowatt hours currently result in related capacity additions at much higher costs. An extreme expression of such contentions is found in the advocacy of inverted rate structures. There is little evidence available, however, that for a rate structure to be cost-related it must have an increasing block character. Such issues can again be decided on the basis of actual figures pertaining to a particular utility and the rates at which it sells electric power. Nevertheless, if one is to take a long run view of rate setting and design, it would be beneficial to see how customers react to different rate structures and the effects of such reactions on fixed costs. For this purpose, the author carried out proper modifications in the dynamic model to introduce declining block rates into the residential sector and carried out simulations to test the effects of changes in the rate structures used.

The rate structures existing in 1974 for residential customers in the Carolina Power and Light region were specified on the basis of data obtained from the North Carolina Utilities Commission. For the three customer groups in this sector, in the relevant range of consumption, these rates in 1974 were

All-electric or high consumption rate group
   for the first 200 KwH per month—$5.80
   for the next 2,300 KwH per month—1.1 cents per KwH
   for additional demand over 2,500 KwH per month—1.0 cents per KwH
Water heater or medium consumption rate group
   for the first 250 KwH per month—$6.75
   for the next 500 KwH per month—1.50 cents per KwH
   for additional demand over 750 KwH per month—1.35 cents per KwH
General or low consumption rate group
   for the first 250 KwH per month—$6.75
   for the next 500 KwH per month—1.50 cents per KwH
   for any additional demand over 750 KwH per month—1.35 cents per KwH

These rates historically have been revised upward by an across-the-board increase in the factor used for multiplying customers' bills calculated every month on the basis of the above rates. This factor at the end of 1974 stood at 1.2795.

In the simulations carried out experimenting with rate structures, the author retained the assumption of a uniform 5.52 percent real increase in prices but with a somewhat different effect. This rate of increase applies to the above mentioned multiplying factor, which was 1.2795 on January 1, 1975. This is different from an increase in price per kilowatt hour at the rate of 5.52 percent, because of the declining block structure of the rates applicable. With changes in quantity of energy consumed, the price per kilowatt hour naturally changes due to this declining block rate structure. The net change between two consecutive periods is, therefore, the cumulative effect of the upward shift in the rate structure itself and the lower price facing the customer with increased consumption. This is similar to the effect described in relation to Figures 1.1 and 1.2. The computer runs were carried out with the following conditions, with rate structure changes taking place wherever indicated with effect from January 1, 1975:

run 1, no change in the rate structure;

run 2, changes made in all three rate groups at the highest block only, so the rates are (a) 2.0 cents per KwH instead of 1.0 cents per KwH for consumption above 2,500 KwH per month for the high consumption group, (b) and (c) 1,85 cents per KwH instead of 1.35 cents per KwH for consumption above 750 KwH for both the mdeium and low consumption groups, respectively;

run 3, in this case the rates for the first 200 KwH in the high consumption group and the first 250 KwH in the medium and low consumption groups, respectively, were kept unchanged; but for steps above these levels, however, all the rates were increased to twice their existing values;

run 4, in this case the highest step in each rate group was eliminated, and only a flat rate above the consumption levels of 200 KwH, 250 KwH, and 250 KwH, respectively, for all three rate groups was extended to apply above these levels. This marginal flat rate was 1.1 cents per KwH, 1.5 cents per KwH, and 1.5 cents per KwH for the three groups, respectively.

Table 8.2 shows the results obtained with these computer runs. Again, annual values for the years 1975, 1980, 1985, and 1990 only have been shown in the table. The results show uniformly the long run effect of higher rate structures on demand in this sector. The largest impact on demand in the residential sector as well as on total net revenues for the whole system is found to take place in run 3, wherein the higher steps consisted of steep rates per kilowatt hour of additional electricity consumed. These rates result in an actual decline in demand in the residential sector between the periods 1975 and 1980. Beyond 1980 there is again an increasing trend, which results in a terminal 1990 value of 8.25 billion kilowatt hours. To the utility, the financial results from run 3 also would appear most favorable, since the net revenues obtained from this set of conditions is the largest of all the alternatives considered. Discussed earlier was the feasibility of introducing steeply rising prices of electricity as a means of improving the finances of an individual utility in the long run.

TABLE 8.2

Effects of Changes in Rate Structure
Applicable to the Residential Sector

Simulation Run	1975	1980	1985	1990
Demand in Residential Sector (in billion KwH)				
Run 1	6.26	7.45	10.34	14.35
Run 2	6.26	7.29	10.15	13.87
Run 3	6.26	5.679	6.122	8.25
Run 4	6.26	7.15	9.91	13.65
Net Revenues (in millions of dollars)				
Run 1	145.3	135.7	192.2	407.7
Run 2	151.9	135.3	197.8	422.9
Run 3	186.2	210.9	247.0	525.4
Run 4	157.6	138.7	198.7	440.0

Source: Compiled by author.

TABLE 8.3

Effect of Revised Rates on Kilowatt Hour
per Customer in the Residential Sector
(in thousands of KwH per customer)

	High Consumption Group	Medium Consumption Group	Low Consumption Group
November-December 1975	2.95	1.71	0.823
November-December 1980	1.80	1.33	0.678
November-December 1985	1.61	1.14	0.812
November-December 1990	1.71	1.34	0.958

Source: Compiled by author.

It is important to consider also the practical effects of steeper rates in relation to the computer simulations now being evaluated. For this purpose values obtained from run 3 only have been tabulated to observe how kilowatt hour per customer will change for each rate group with the inputs used in run 3. These are shown for the periods November-December in 1975, 1980, 1985, and 1990, respectively, in Table 8.3.

The figures in Table 8.3 show that the decline in kilowatt hour per customer is by no means unusually drastic. In fact, in the general or low consumption rate group there is actually an increase in kilowatt hour per customer between 1975 and 1990. The gap in this variable for each of the three groups narrows considerably in response to the rates introduced. This naturally would reduce the extent of cross-subsidization between high consumption and low consumption customers and thus achieve one of the objectives of good rate design.

The modifications made in the dynamic model and the simulations attempted from it as described would indicate that a modification of rate structures is an effective policy tool for achieving desired objectives in the long run. The prime objective of using precise cost-related rates, when not attained, leads to economic inefficiencies and inequitable allocation of costs between customers buying electricity. Where such inefficiencies and cross-subsidization exist, appropriate changes in existing rate structures can eliminate them effectively in the long run.

NOTE

1. Robert W. Llewellyn, FORDYN, An Industrial Dynamics Simulator (Raleigh, N. C.: private publication, 1965).

CHAPTER

9

THE CASE FOR GOVERNMENT ASSISTANCE

In keeping with a familiar trend observed with large U.S. industries, a period of financial problems always provides the setting for calls seeking assistance from the federal government. In the case of the electric utility industry, the very nature of the product supplied by it and the record of close regulation by public agencies adds momentum to such calls during the "energy" crisis facing the industry. Increasing blame for the financial ill health of the investor-owned electric utilities in the United States is being directed toward regulators and the regulatory process. This is not without justification, since the regulatory process always has reacted with considerable tardiness, which is being felt increasingly with rapidly escalating costs.

The main thesis of the paper by Paul Joskow and Paul MacAvoy[1] is based on a critical look at the flaws in the regulatory process as it exists today. The authors have quantified the future shortfall in financing abilities of U.S. investor-owned electric utilities and pointed to prompt price increases, unhampered by regulatory restraints as a possible solution toward ensuring long run stability of the industry.

The economic events of the mid-1970s have induced a feeling of helplessness in the electric utility industry, and there is serious questioning of the industry's own capacity to solve its problems. A great part of the blame for the mess is being directed to the government. Utility officials point a finger at the federal government with the sort of attitude that could be expressed in, "You got us into this mess—now get us out of it."

The electric utility industry is a huge giant. A proposal for any type of federal assistance must be evaluated carefully since its repercussions would be felt throughout the entire economy. Political expediency should have no place in any decision to grant subsidies, and yet no individual or group can deny that a serious problem exists to which solutions have to be found very soon. In a speech reported by the Washington Post on March 25, 1975, Secretary of the Interior Rogers C. B. Morton proposed that the federal government subsidize the electric power industry on a temporary basis. His proposals included, "Loan guarantees and other goverment financing mechanisms; additional changes in the tax treatment of utility stock dividends; rebates on oil taxes and import fees; and cash rebates of unused investment tax credits." He also told his audience, "I can promise you early decisions on further measures we have under consideration." This line of thinking was justified by him on the grounds that "were it not for the extraordinary events of the past year and a half—and the shocking effects of these events on the electric utility in particular— I would not be advocating any federal involvement. But we must be realistic—you do need help."

In the light of this expression of Washington's position on subsidies, one has some indication of what measures could be implemented. However, some comments on other related proposals also would be in order, for this issue is likely to remain the subject of lively debate in the years to come. If the order in which Morton listed his proposals is any indication of the priorities assigned to each of them by the executive branch of the federal government, then the one likely to be implemented first is what is known as the Rosenberg plan (named after William G. Rosenberg, the chairman of the Michigan Public Service Commission).

Under the Rosenberg plan there would be a program of government-guaranteed loans, which the electric companies could draw on at the interest rates paid on government securities. The need for such loans would be established by the state regulatory agency concerned. A modification of this plan proposes the government should make loans available at interest rates lower than those prevailing in the market.

Another suggestion that has gained wide support in electric utility circles is to establish a body patterned after the Reconstruction Finance Corporation (RFC) of 1932, but with a narrower scope confined only to aiding the electric utility industry. A variation of this proposal advocates the establishment of a cooperative bank run by the utilities, more or less on the lines of rural electrification cooperatives.

In an article on electric utilities in Business Week,[2] Shearon Harris, chairman of Carolina Power and Light, was quoted as proposing that the U.S. government slash utilities' income tax requirements, allow them to claim half their common stock dividends as expenses, and guarantee a rate of return for a new class of preferred stock. D. Bruce Mansfield, who favors the establishment of a RFC-type corporation, also wants a three-year moratorium on income taxes. His hope is that "such actions would not lead to nationalization."[3]

But nationalization, too, is an issue that is currently being talked about. Theodore E. Maynard, president of National Utilitiy Service, Incorporated, a consulting firm active in this field, has stated that "Electricity is so basic, that the profit motive should be taken out."[4]

The issue of nationalization apart, all other schemes mentioned above amount to a direct or indirect subsidy of electric utilities by the taxpayer. The peculiarities of the current situation indicate that a sole reliance on the free market to solve the problems of the industry would warrant a long period of adjustment and turmoil, during which there would be considerable dislocation in living styles and economic activities. But a subsidy of any form would have adverse effects too. These have been voiced, among others, by Murray L. Weidenbaum in the autumn 1974 issue of **Financial Management**.[5]

The general argument against governmental assistance is, understandably, that such action does not draw on any new source of capital for the economy as a whole but merely reallocates funds to one industry by diverting them from other industries. Weidenbaum contends that empirical evidence indicates that federal credit programs do not increase the total flow of either savings or investment. According to him, it is not the large corporation that will be rationed out with this reallocation of funds but mainly state and local governments, medium-sized and smaller businesses, private mortgage borrowers, and consumers. Another drawback, mentioned in connection with the Rosenberg plan but obviously existent with any kind of public subsidy, is incentive to minimize high-risk undertakings.

Rosenberg, who has been emphasizing the merits of his plan in recent conferences and meetings, counters the fear of macroeconomic inefficiency by citing the examples of other industries that have been the beneficiaries of some form of government assistance or other. In an FEA-sponsored Electricity Rate Conference held in Washington, D. C., on June 19, 1974, he drew attention to various forms of tax credits, investment credits, and depletion allowances amounting to over $6.00 billion a year, which energy companies have been getting over a long period. An interesting point made by Rosenberg was that loans made by the Export-Import Bank are for financing of electric and other energy projects in countries as diverse as Algeria, Japan, and Russia. Rosenberg contends that financing domestic energy projects will have no different or adverse economic effects from those associated with foreign projects.

Through all the pages being written on both sides of the government assistance controversy, there is a conspicuous absence of one element—there is little or no attempt to estimate the long run nature of the industry's financial problems. By and large most suggestions being put forward represent a reaction to the current crisis. On the other hand, there is no serious attempt in most quarters to assess the long run effects of subsidies on the industry's future operations themselves.

CASE FOR GOVERNMENT ASSISTANCE 161

The discussions presented in the previous chapters reveal three clear features in the long run problem of electric utility finances:

(1) A judiciously devised scheme of price increases would be required to reduce growth in demand, boost net revenues, and yet be acceptable to an increasingly irate body of consumers.

(2) Cost increases must be controlled effectively. Whereas some cost-related factors are beyond the control of the utilities themselves, one of them in particular, namely that of correct investment decisions, needs close and enlightened management.

(3) If appropriate actions related to the above two features are taken promptly and sustained in the years to come, the capital requirements of the industry would present a problem only for the next few years. All the simulations carried out in this study indicate a definite pattern of behavior of the system in the years to come. In spite of the variety of assumptions used, the dynamic path of financial variables exhibited qualitatively similar trends in all the results obtained.

Taking a long run view of the future of demand and supply in this country's electrical energy sector, the problem only reduces to a short run problem of a shortage of finances at existing prices. This author would, on these grounds, look with disfavor on all suggestions for federal assistance being voiced around the country. The biggest flaw in these schemes lies in the encouragement they would provide to increase demand in the long run, thereby leading to a misallocation of resources in the economy. Increases in demand, when anticipated, will continue to spur a high rate of construction activity resulting in an augmented supply potential in the industry. A large capital base and excess capacity, therefore, will ensue from federal support and continue to exert the pressures that are bringing about such actions now in the first place. In other words, a misallocation of resources, if permitted in a vital industry such as this, would most likely remain a millstone around the neck of policy makers in Washington, D. C.

The above remarks should not be taken to suggest that no government action in the electrical energy arena is recommended. The government has a large role to play in promoting efficient solutions where significant divergences exist between private and social costs and private and social benefits. Subsidies may be considered for bringing about greater coordination between electric utilities, on the basis that private marginal benefits from coordination historically have been much too small to justify the costs a utility would have to incur to achieve it. In the aggregate, however, the benefits to the nation as a whole perhaps would justify a modest expense by the taxpayer. Informational costs and institutional constraints related to the region-based character of the electric utility industry have been a barrier to achieving an economically optimum degree of coordination in the United States.

A stronger case than that for coordination can be made for government subsidies for research and development; government participation and entry into the field will not suffice. A case can be made for greater efforts by the utilities themselves using the advantages they possess by virtue of their involvement at the base of the industry's operations. Such efforts, particularly in the field of energy-related regional economics, will have large spin-off benefits for the entire nation, justifying contributions by the public exchequer. Some of the actions of the FEA inspire optimism on all these fronts.

NOTES

1. Paul Joskow and Paul W. MacAvoy, "Shifts in the Electric Power Industry," paper presented at the Allied Social Science Association's Annual Meeting, San Francisco, California, December 1974.

2. "Utilities: Weak Point in the Energy Future," Business Week, January 20, 1975.

3. Ibid.

4. Ibid.

5. Morris L. Weidenbaum, "The Case Against Government Guarantees of Electric Utility Bonds," Financial Management

CHAPTER

10

THE OUTLOOK FOR THE UNITED STATES

It is difficult to gaze into a crystal ball and paint a picture of the future in any endeavor, even more so when the crystal ball is dimly lit. Not since the depression, and perhaps even longer, has there been such an atmosphere of gloom in electric utility circles. But scientific investigation and research have no place for being overwhelmed by this manifestation of gloom, and any prognosis made for the industry's future must be carefully based on an objective analysis of the strengths, weaknesses, and long run characteristics of the system on which the industry rests.

In this study the whole has been explained by trying to dissect a part in such a way that the total electric utility industry in the United States can be understood by baring the working of a regional system. It is of interest to observe that one of the best-managed utilities in the nation is being tested by a combination of severe problems, and this should be an indication of the seriousness of the crisis gripping the entire industry. A study of the dynamics of electric utility operations as presented in this book also should suggest some tools for reasonable speculations on the direction in which the industry is moving. In doing so it would, therefore, be rational to sum up the dynamic long run trends observed within the system and how these are likely to be affected by possible developments exogenous to the system.

The first aspect that merits attention in any analysis of the electric power industry in the United States is that related to the cost of inputs. To a large degree the 1974-75 crisis is the result of sharp, unexpected increases in those costs. The first comment that one can make about costs is that, in general, they are likely to continue increasing at rates higher than the historical average. Even the administration's own predictions, made known in early 1975, specify increases in the Consumer price index of 11.3 percent, 7,8 percent, and 6.6 percent for the years 1975-77. Thus, construction costs will continue to go up at an annual rate that would depend largely on the national and global demand for generating equipment. The September 1973 issue of Nuclear Engineering International[1] published a survey of the world market for commerical nuclear power plants. The predictions made therein indicate that demands for nuclear power plants will continue to grow at considerably higher rates than experienced so far. Yet, at the same time, cost reductions due to technological improvements, greater experience in construction, and standardization of component parts are likely to take place. The overall outlook for nuclear plant capital costs in the future appears to be fairly uncertain at present, but there appears no reason for unusually large increases in the future. The costs of conventional generating plants also are on the increase, the greatest uncertainty in this regard being related to costs of pollution control equipment. Further, limited cost reductions in these plants now appear possible, since technical improvements are either not feasible or uneconomical with current knowledge. At any rate, the large scale shift toward nuclear generating capacity would make the cost of fossil-fuel based plants unimportant in the future.

Whereas we would not expect capital costs of plants in the future expansion plans to deviate substantially from 1975 levels, the main uncertainty for the industry lies in future fuel costs. Events since the 1973 Yom Kippur War have made predicting oil prices a difficult undertaking since these are, to a large extent, now dependent on the actions of the Organization of Petroleum Exporting Countries (OPEC) cartel. Recent trends in oil consumption and the strains being felt by the cartel point to a probable era of stable prices. A careful study of issues involved in determining United States and world oil prices as aired in the recent collection of essays, The Energy Question, edited by Edward Erickson and Leonard Waverman,[2] leaves the impression that the oil cartel now effectively controlling oil prices cannot continue to do so indefinitely. In fact in the view of some experts a drop in world oil prices is merely a question of time. This outlook has interesting implications for generating capacity additions. In the present value computations presented in Part II of this book, it was noted that over the horizon extending to 1990, the present value of conventional generation was lower than that of nuclear generation. If the electric power industry continues to flounder in financially rough seas and there occurs a drop in oil prices, it is not unlikely that a shift back to fossil-fuel based plant additions may take place. In that case the federal government's actions may have to be directed toward either providing incentives for constructing nuclear plants or legislating against construction of new fossil-fuel capacity. The aggregate effect of new conventional plant construction in the United States would again bring about greater dependence in oil on foreign sources of supply. This may not be acceptable to both the executive and legislative branches of government.

It would be useful at the same time to consider, on the other hand, a not so optimistic scenario in future oil prices. If the oil cartel were able to control oil prices for an extended duration, prices could rise at least at the general rate of inflation in the industrialized nations of the West, and possibly somewhat higher. This would be reflected in higher electricity prices in the United States. The most ominous aspect of any such success for the OPEC countries would be its effects on other suppliers and the danger this poses in pricing of other fuels—most notably for future uranium supplies.

In the January 15, 1975, issue of Forbes,[3] a disconcerting report has been presented on the possibility of a strong OPEC-type uranium cartel emerging in the next few years. Unlike the oil cartel, the uranium producing countries have been conducting their meetings unobtrusively and in strict secrecy. The first meeting of the so-called Uranium Producers Forum was held in May 1972 in Johannesburg, South Africa; and participants to this were representing uranium interest in Britain, Canada, Australia, France, and South Africa. Since then some signs have been observed indicating a reduction of competitiveness in the uranium market. In fact, most foreign suppliers are currently writing contracts with price clauses such as "world price at time of delivery," pointing to an implied expectation of higher prices in the future. The vulnerability of the electric power industry to price setting in uranium cannot be explained in terms of costs alone. Even at $20 a pound, uranium costs would be only 14 percent of the price of electricity, against 72 percent for oil at $12 a barrel. Even large price increases in uranium would, therefore, have an inappreciable impact on electricity price. The danger from cartelization, however, lies in precisely this fact—the relatively small share of uranium in electricity prices gives the uranium cartel considerable scope for large price increases without attracting excessive attention, and this may result in a largely nuclear based generating capacity being held to ransom by a small, cohesive group of suppliers.

It is well known that the United States has vast reserves of uranium, but these are not being tapped as rapidly as the growth in demand. The process of locating new deposits and setting up mining equipment to extract the ore takes up to eight years. United States companies are not expanding domesitc operations, since most of them are still working on contracts averaging out to $11 a pound in 1980. This makes it economically desirable to wait until prices increase before expanding supplies in the U.S. market. In the meantime, demand is estimated to triple by 1980 and increase by 700 percent by 1985. Even if there is large scale postponement or cancellation of new nuclear plant construction, demand will expand rapidly enough to make price setting in uranium a strong possibility. The dynamics of the market suggest that price increases based on cartel decisions could start making an impact around 1978 or 1979. According to Robert Ninninger, an official of the Atomic Energy Commission (AEC), "The tight supply situation may hit a little later than 1979, but once it does hit, the problem will last forever. It might be relieved when we get breeder reactors, but they won't have a significant impact until the latter part of the century or later."[4]

Whereas situations such as the above may have no solutions short of political actions over the next 20 years or so, preparations could be made in this period for developing alternatives in generation that would have widespread commercial application at least by the turn of the century. The most promising of these alternatives appears to be the development of the fast breeder reactor. A detailed study of the economics of developing nuclear breeder reactors was published by Paul MacAvoy,[5] in which he determined the present values of costs and benefits associated with different types of projects under development. He identified the best strategy to be pursued as one that would depend on the budgetary constraints imposed on the projects being evaluated and the objectives that should guide their execution. His recommendation was, however, that programs should be under way to develop liquid metal fast breeder reactors and gas fast breeders of all size classes, and that there should be a policy of duplicating projects and programs in different companies and technologies.

The United States, by virtue of its dominance in the nuclear field, had an early lead in development of breeder reactors; but other nations have either caught up or passed us, at least in the area of power plant construction. Great resources and attention are now being directed to the United States' Clinch River Demonstration Plant, which is scheduled for start-up in 1980. Availability of fast breeder reactors on a commercial scale probably will not be evident before the 1990s Therefore, there are few indications on likely future costs of electricity generated by fast breeder reactor plants. All that can be said is that there is a promise of this type of reactor being more efficient and economical than the light water reactor plants in use and under construction at present.

Another significant element of cost in this analysis is the cost of capital. Financial problems are compounded further by higher costs of borrowing in the market. Government assistance may reduce these to an appreciable extent in the future, but in the absence of such action, capital costs are likely to keep on increasing for at least the next five or six years, beyond which price increases may bring about an improvement in net revenues. The simulations in this regard were based on the premise of constant costs in real terms, which may be somewhat optimistic. If costs increase substantially, price increases cannot be made large enough for political and practical reasons; and the financial health of the industry definitely would warrant blood transfusions in the form of governmental assistance.

The issue of pricing is going to be critical to the growth and stability of the electric utility industry in the future. Prices of electiricity and the rate structures that are in use cannot any longer be regarded as an area for across-the-board increases. The prices of electricity—determined by the rates that are offered to customers— have by far the most important direct effects on demand and indirect effects on the decisions to bring about or the ability to finance the augmentation of generating capacity. It is therefore evident that a new era for pricing of electric power in this country is at hand. Signs of radical change already can be seen in the actions of some regulatory commissions.

The New York Times of December 8, 1974, described a landmark in utility rate regulation. The Wisconsin Public Service Commission in August 1974 ordered the Madison Gas and Electric Company to revise its rate structure to a flat form, by throwing out the traditional declining block structure. In doing so, the commission also adopted the principles of incremental cost pricing of energy as the "touchstones" of its rate regulation policy. More regulators are now insisting on "cost of service" studies before granting rate increases to price electricity to customers in accordance with the full costs of supplying it. In a historical departure from past practice the North Carolina Utilities Commission in the rate revision granted to Carolina Power and Light effective January 6, 1975, did not allow an across-the-board increase in rates but made the price per kilowatt hour more expensive for higher consumption blocks for certain classes of customers. With the generation of electric power becoming more capital-intensive, the fixed cost component of electricity costs is becoming larger; and, therefore, customers whose demands for energy impose larger fixed costs on the system should not be able to buy successive units of power at decreasing costs. In years to come, the regulation of the industry will require changes in rate structures to bring electricity prices in line with the long run incremental cost principle.

The regulatory process also will exhibit change in the regulatory lag, which has been observed historically in the grant of rate increases. The desire to cut down on delays in rate revision cases is evident in the widespread use of the fuel price escalator clause. The adverse effect of regulatory practices is brought out clearly in the paper mentioned earlier by Paul Joskow and Paul MacAvoy.[6] In principle, this author agrees with the main thrust of their arguments, but the static assumptions used for growth in demand in their model seem somewhat high and inflexible. All indications from the simulations described in this model show that, with a modest rate of price increases, the growth in future demand will be much lower than experienced in the late 1960s. Hence, price increases must be viewed in relation to their long run effect on demand.

That the procedures used in regulation must undergo substantial change is an imperative. But policies that all those connected with the electric utility industry pursue must go beyond making improvements in the existing institutions only. A judicious mix of different policies is necessary to achieve objectives that will ensure long run supplies of electricity when demanded at prices that do not result in severe problems of adjustment for all types of customers. The approach being advocated by the Federal Energy Administration (FEA) is in keeping with the conclusions reached in this particular study. The FEA approach was outlined by Donald B. Craven, associate assistant administrator, in a speech delivered in Washington, D. C. on October 7, 1974. This approach required three types of action:

> First, reduce the growth in demand for electricity, and improve its efficiency.
> Second, coordinate a federal program that combines the elements of increased research and development support, tax policy changes and streamlined environmental measures.
> Third, revise state regulatory practices to meet the changed utilities needs.[7]

Reduction of growth in demand is of vital importance. The effects of prices are such that revenues are increased in the long run and demand considerably reduced. Craven estimates that a reduction in annual growth rate for the United States to 5 percent from about 7 percent would reduce capital requirements by more than one quarter while projected revenues are cut by only 6 percent. The results from our simulation results reveal similar benefits from increasing prices. As an extension of this concept, seasonal pricing schemes also were found to be efficient in reducing long run capital requirements for the utility. There is a strong case for implementing seasonal pricing schemes in the future, and the concept is bound to spread once satisfactory results have been obtained in one region. In this regard, the project to test the effects of various rate structures during the peak load winter season (currently under experiment at the Green Mountain Power Company) is being watched carefully by utilities around the nation. Hence in the years to come, one might see a number of innovations in seasonal pricing and, perhaps, with design and manufacture of appropriate metering devices, a move toward time-of-day metering.

This latter system uses the same principle as the seasonal pricing schemes, except that variations in price apply to different hours of the day to inhibit large energy use in hours of peak demand.

To those in the industry concerned with the question "Will investor-owned public utilities survive?" precise answers seem to be elusive. It is feared that the analysis presented in this book also would prove inadequate in providing a definite answer, which is as it should be. The author merely has attempted to expose the behavior of the system as a whole and has traced out some of the dynamic effects of policy actions and events within a quantitative framework. There are too many imponderables in the situation to allow a definite prediction of events within the industry. Two aspects of the situation, however, leave room enough for guarded optimism.

First, the crisis gripping electric utilities is symptomatic of the entire electric power business in the United States. Proponents of the view that small municipally managed systems or large government-owned systems are the answer to our electrical energy problems have been dismayed by events and developments in the public sector of the industry. A case in point is the current ills of the Tennessee Valley Authority, the huge dynamo of power in the nation's industrial workshop; that utility was often displayed as a model of efficient functioning in the electric power market. Even now, TVA has certain advantages that other utilities do not enjoy. For instance, it has been able to borrow money at under 8 percent interest rates from the Federal Financing Bank when the open market rate was nearly 11 percent. It also still has a tax advantage, being required to pay only 5 percent of its revenues from nonfederal sales to local communities, as against investor-owned utilities paying almost twice that percentage in taxes. Yet, the April 1, 1975 issue of Forbes[8] indicates that the industry's problems have not spared the government's colossus, which has been the subject of rapid rate increases, forced cutbacks in power supply, difficulties in raising capital for construction, and more—all typical of the general situation prevailing in the industry. Municipal power systems too are in no better shape financially, although the impact of their problems has not been felt widely on account of their relatively small size.

Publicly owned power, for these reasons, does not seem to offer prospects any brighter than those of private ownership, an opinion that seems to be shared in Washington, D. C. Purely on a political plane, therefore, the fact of uniform distress within the industry is likely to result in help from the government within the existing institutional arrangement of ownership. The actions already proposed by the administration, if passed, will be of significant benefit to the industry.

The second reason for guarded optimism is provided by an analysis of the factors that have brought about financial turmoil in electric utilities. Far too many changes have taken place at the same time, for which neither the regulating agencies nor the managements of electric utilities were prepared institutionally. The article in Business Week[9] mentions, "The electric utility industry is hardly known for dynamic leadership." Forecasting techniques used by some utilities have been woefully primitive, requiring nothing more than mere extrapolation of trends. Investment plans once made are regarded as sacrosanct; and even now, in the wake of considerable slowdown in growth of demand, postponements and cancellations of planned projects are being made with funereal sorrow. A change in management philosophy will come about after considerable deliberation and delay. Even the relatively better-managed utilities in the meantime will continue groping for solutions and a helping hand from the government.

In this author's view, if government help or even the promise of minimal help can keep electric utilities solvent in the next two or three years, better times will follow. Demand trends would by then be established more firmly, and this may lead to more decisive and bolder action by utility executives in slowing down capital expenditures. There is also a likelihood of improvements in the regulatory process itself, granting utilities prompter rate increases to enable realization of fair rates of return. This can already be seen in the financial results of some utilities for the first quarter of 1975. Carolina Power and Light announced earnings per share for the period ending March 31, 1975, of $2.38 and net income of $84.8 million, against $2.29 and $72 million, respectively, for the same period last year. Virginia Electric and Power Company announced earnings per share for the period ending March 31, 1975, of $1.69, against $1.62 for the year ending December 21, 1974. In the early 1980s, there is every indication that there will be a strong upward trend in the financial fortunes of the industry. This is based on results from the computer simulations described in earlier chapters.

One swallow does not make a summer; there are hazards in writing on the outlook for the entire United States based on a study of one utility, but perhaps no more so than in measuring the cost of living on the basis of selected commodities included in the consumer price index. Besides, the region used in the model suffers from problems that are typical of the industry; the differences are merely a matter of degree. The dynamic forces acting on each utility are qualitatively similar, and, therefore, there is reason to believe that the long run effect of these factors, too, would be somewhat uniform.

There is some satisfaction for an author starting a book on a note of pessimism and ending it somewhat optimistically. Accordingly, an optimistic posture is appropriate at this stage. The future of the electric utility industry appears difficult but not dismal. With the smugness that comes of accomplishing an arduous job, it can also be said that the dynamics of electrical energy can be explained easily on the basis of elementary price theory. But that again is as it should be, for one is then reminded and reassured that it is all there in Alfred Marshall or Adam Smith or John Hicks.

NOTES

1. "The World Market for Commerical Nuclear Plant," Nuclear Engineering International (September 1973).

2. Edward W. Erickson and Leonard Waverman, eds., The Energy Question (Toronto, Canada: The University of Toronto Press, 1974).

3. "The Uranium Cartel," Forbes, January 15, 1975.

4. Ibid.

5. Paul W. MacAvoy, Economic Strategy for Developing Nuclear Breeder Reactors (Cambridge, Mass.: The Massachusetts Institute of Technology Press, 1969).

6. Paul Joskow and Paul W. MacAvoy, "Shifts in the Electric Power Industry," paper presented at the Allied Social Science Association's Annual Meeting, San Francisco, California, December 1974.

7. Craven, Donald B., address before conference on "Current Trends in Public Utility Financing and Accounting," October 7, 1974, Washington, D.C.

8. "Tennessee Valley Authority," Forbes, April, 1975.

9. "Utilities: Weak Point in the Energy Future," Business Week, January 20, 1975.

ABOUT THE AUTHOR

R. K. PACHAURI is currently assistant professor in the Department of Economics and Business at the North Carolina State University, Raleigh. The author has had extensive industrial experience both on this continent and in India, and has conducted industry studies related to the manufacture of electrical generating equipment and electrical metering instruments.

Dr. Pachauri holds a Ph D. in economics and industrial engineering and a master of science degree in industrial engineering, both from North Carolina State University at Raleigh. He is also a graduate of the Institution of Production Engineers, London.

RELATED TITLES
Published by
Praeger Special Studies

COOPERATIVE RURAL ELECTRIFICATION: Case
Studies of the Pilot Projects in Latin America
James E. Ross

PLANT SIZE, TECHNOLOGICAL CHANGE, AND
INVESTMENT REQUIREMENTS: A Dynamic Framework
for the Long-Run Average Cost Curve
David Huettner

THE SOVIET ENERGY BALANCE: Natural Gas, Other
Fossil Fuels, and Alternative Power Sources
Iain F. Elliot